Aubrey Wilson's Marketing Audit Check Lists

Aubrey Wilson's Marketing Audit Check Lists

A guide to effective
marketing resource realization

McGRAW-HILL Book Company (UK) Limited

London · New York · St Louis · San Francisco · Auckland
Bogotá · Guatemala · Hamburg · Johannesburg · Lisbon · Madrid
Mexico · Montreal · New Delhi · Panama · Paris · San Juan
São Paulo · Singapore · Sydney · Tokyo · Toronto

Published by
McGRAW-HILL Book Company (UK) Limited
MAIDENHEAD · BERKSHIRE · ENGLAND

British Library Cataloguing in Publication Data
Wilson, Aubrey
  Aubrey Wilson's marketing audit check lists.
  1. Marketing audits   2. Marketing management
  I. Title
  658.8′3   HF5412.2

  ISBN 0-07-084574-3

Library of Congress Cataloging in Publication Data
Wilson, Aubrey.
  Aubrey Wilson's marketing audit check lists.
  Includes index.
  1. Marketing audits.   I. Title.
HF5415.16.W53   658.8′02   81-20741
ISBN 0-07-084574-3   AACR2

1 2 3 4 5 JWA 8 5 4 3 2

Filmset in 'Monophoto' Times and Univers
by Eta Services (Typesetters) Ltd., Beccles, Suffolk
Printed in Great Britain by
Spottiswoode Ballantyne Ltd. Colchester and London

To Penny with all my love

Contents

Preface

It is not surprising that the turbulent conditions which typified the 1970s and the even more unpredictable environment forecast for the 1980s have caused considerable retrenchment within companies. When it comes to cost cutting, high on the list of expendable activities come all forms of marketing, particularly advertising and PR, market research and exhibitions. While it cannot be denied that there is much waste in these and other marketing activities, wholesale amputation is as unnecessary as it is dangerous. Companies under stress tend to go for the surgeon's knife before considering physiotherapy!

There is, in most organizations, a considerable marketing resource either not utilized, under-utilized or utilized incorrectly. It only requires a realization of what is available for any sentient businessman to be able to adjust his activities so as to exploit fully what is already possessed. However, making an inventory, mostly qualitative, is both difficult and time-consuming and, moreover, has strong internal political connotations. There is little wonder that the assessment of marketing resources and their utilizations is rarely undertaken methodically. This book is an attempt to rectify such a situation.

The genesis of the technique that is described and explained in the book sprang originally from the need, at the start of a marketing research project, to establish just what data the sponsors already possessed and the degree of confidence that could be placed in their reliability. Very considerable sums of money and an inordinate amount of time were frequently wasted on searching for information that did in fact exist but had not been extracted.

Thus a list of key, if somewhat general, questions was developed for use at the beginning of any research project. However, it became increasingly obvious in studying the answers to many of the questions that most firms could materially improve their performance by a greater exploitation of both the information and the marketing resources they already possessed. Consequently, the check lists, which were originally market data-orientated, were considerably extended to cover all aspects of a company's marketing activities.

The answers to the questions, individually and in combination, lead quickly to recommendations for a series of basic actions which lead to impressive achievements. This approach has been described as a return to fundamentalism in marketing. Instead of theories, elegant plans, sophisticated strategies and esoteric philosophies, it produced down-to-earth practical suggestions which could, for most organizations, be implemented at once at no cost or low cost. There was no magic in this: it was simply using fully or re-deploying what a business already possessed.

The marketing resource realization technique, for that is what it is, has now been used many times and has never failed to produce operational and thus profit improvements—sometimes marginal, sometimes substantial, but always justifying the time investment in the audit.

This is not the first book to be written on marketing audits, and all claim to be practical. No one, however, has sought to provide a comprehensive model of information requirements, or to formulate them in such a way that the answers suggest the sources of action to be followed. The purpose of this book is to provide a methodological approach to the identification, collection, and evaluation of the marketing resources and strengths and weaknesses of a company; to exploit the former and avoid the latter where they cannot be corrected. It is hoped that its essential value will be the bringing together of the accumulated experiences, good and bad, of the many individuals and organizations involved in a wide range of industries and services, and with different levels of marketing and sales sophistication or primitivism, with which the author has had the privilege of working in over 30 years of intense involvement in marketing. The book has no national connotations. The technique and the questions can be (and have) applied from Kenya to Canada and from Australia to Iceland.

It would be a very arrogant author who would claim that any marketing book is entirely his own work. The very nature of marketing precludes any such claim as all authors and practitioners must lean heavily on the triumphs and failures of their predecessors. This book hopefully draws on the lessons of both.

It will be seen that the technique of marketing resources realization or marketing auditing could not have sprung fully grown from the womb. It has been evolved empirically from a wholly practical base—within companies. The check list audit approach was originally devised for Redman Heenan International, whose chairman, Angus Murray, provided not only the encouragement but also the opportunity to develop it by applying it to many of his group companies. David Rowles, managing director, Heenan Environmental Systems, was always available to give much wise advice, particularly in how to motivate managers to exploit the results of the audit. I must also acknowledge the role of Brian Gould, now managing director, Warwick Engineering, for both tactfully ignoring some of the stranger aberrations that came out of the early audits and for suggesting further lines of development.

Richard Skinner, marketing director of Reliance Systems, meticulously examined the early lists, and his many suggestions and amendments removed much that was obscure and ambiguous, thereby both lightening and speeding the task of the auditor. Michael Rines, the editor-in-chief of *Marketing*, saw a value in giving the lists a much wider exposure to encourage firms to undertake their own marketing audits and to create an internal capability rather than an external dependency on specialists. He was enthusiastic enough to persuade me not only to publish them as a part of a weekly series, but also to write commentaries which, as events have turned out and judging by the response from *Marketing* readers, have proved to be highly relevant in guiding auditors in their interpretations.

The series produced many suggestions for additions and changes, most of which have been incorporated. As a result, each section is now about twice as long as the original and the commentaries have also been considerably extended.

Mrs Mary Griffin, special director, Smiths Industries, has always given generously of her time and depth of knowledge. In particular, many of the ideas in List 15, 'Introducing new products/services', and diagrams were developed by her. Adopting the role of auditor, she read the manuscript to see how easy or difficult it was to administer and how well it worked. This role-playing lead to a number of very important changes. Scarred perhaps by too many products of the 'easy-to-assemble' category, she was determined that this would not be the sort of do-it-yourself approach that needs an MBA and many years in consultancy to undertake.

I must thank Mrs Jan Bennett, who somehow sorted out the incredible 'scissors and pasting' and idiosyncratic numbering and section-linking system in order to get the manuscript into a comprehensible state. Only by obtaining an understanding of the audit technique was she able to do this, and I am grateful that her interest was such that she willingly studied the lists as well as typing them. The final manuscript with its very consider-able and important cross referencing was immaculately prepared by Mrs Ann Wooster in an incredibly short period of time.

This is the seventh marketing book I have published. Each one has been based on practical experience in marketing and owes little to academic research or approaches which I have frequently criticized. Academics' lack of constant and practical involvement in marketing has distanced them from the daily problems and management education, it has been well stated, 'has become badly out of touch with the real world of business'.[1] In a world where survival takes precedence over growth, there is little time for elegance and sophistication of the expansive 'sixties'. The contribution I hope this book will make will be a return to fundamentalism in marketing and a rapid measurable improvement in the operations and security of the firms that adopt the approach.

1. 'The decline of management ethics', *Journal of General Management*, Spring issue 1981, Henley.

The marketing audit

A self-administered method for identifying and realizing under-utilized marketing resources

The 'marketing audit' has become a sort of 'buzz' phrase in the very recent past although few people have attempted to codify it. One well-known marketing audit check list by a leading American guru smacks more of the tabloids' pseudo-psychological tests of the 'are you a great lover?' type, where given scores indicate the level of proficiency. Making a marketing audit on this basis may be amusing—indeed, may be useful in a philosophic sense—but it has very little down-to-earth practical application.

The answer to the question, 'Does management recognize the importance of designing the company to serve the needs and wants of chosen markets?' is difficult to translate into immediate practical actions.

What is attempted in this book is to bring together the technique of the marketing audit with the technique of the check list approach. The value of check lists is substantially three-fold: (1) not to have to re-think, re-order and re-write what has perhaps been done many times before; (2) to be able to obtain an insight into the thinking and experience of others in the same field; and (3) to ensure that no important item is forgotten. Whether a check list is used simply for packing for a holiday or is a complex one such as might be used in a nuclear power station, the advantages and the uses remain the same. The check list approach to marketing provides a reliable short-cut in assembling information and an insurance that within the broad span that comprises corporate policy no vital issue or question is omitted.

It is recognized that check lists can also inhibit original thinking and produce an unconsidered acceptance of what has been presented. The lists that follow are only a starting point—a logical notation of aspects of the firm's operations which impact on marketing strategy and marketing actions. To be fully effective they not only require screening and re-orientating; they also require expanding to meet the needs of the auditor, the activities and aspirations of his organizations.

Apart from providing clear guidelines as to the actions, a company might undertake to improve its position. The check lists, used correctly as an audit guide, have the inestimable advantage of identifying and utilizing marketing resources of every type. The reason why these are not fully exploited is not difficult to understand. Many firms do not know what resources they own or their quality. Frequently, because of received wisdom, old practices and habits and sometimes despair, they are constrained from introducing simple changes which would release much of the currently under-exploited resources the company possesses.

The author has found that many practical suggestions, which might be termed at no higher level than 'hot tips', will emerge from the audit. They may lack the elegance of sophisticated marketing strategies and systems, but they have the overwhelming advantage of being practical, immediate and most frequently no cost or of low cost.

That is not to suggest that marketing systems and marketing strategies are irrelevant. Nothing could be further from the truth. Indeed, the random, disconnected ideas that will develop might well be a test in themselves as to the practicality of the marketing systems and organization and the marketing plan. Any recommendations that derive from the audit should be considered both on their own merit and in relation to other corporate activities—marketing and non-marketing. They form yet another usable and desirable outcome of the methodical, step-by-step approach inherent in all well composed check lists.

The marketing audit, unlike many benchmark studies, does have a value as a one-off free-standing exercise, but its greatest use is as an on-going regular practice of the company, so that comparison can be made between the results of each audit. Very early on (List 1, 'Marketing strategy and planning') emphasis is placed on clear and agreed objectives. As the Cheshire Cat pointed out, if you do not know where you are going, 'it doesn't matter which way you go'. It will not take a marketing audit to decide if the objectives have been achieved, but the audit will show if the route chosen was the most effective and profitable. It will also indicate whether particular marketing activities are better intensified, adjusted or dropped.

Attention is drawn to both the obvious and the esoteric, which will be different for each firm and manager. Thus, some questions may seem simple and indeed primitive for one organization or person while the same points in another context may represent totally new thoughts.

Not surprisingly, most marketing check lists are externally orientated and do not take into account the strengths and weaknesses of the company or the resources available over any period of time. While this book is substantially and intentionally inward-looking, and is designed to highlight the issues specific to a company and those that impact on marketing, it has by no means ignored the external situation.

That is not to say that most managers do not know a great deal about their company, have a lively knowledge of the immediate environments in which they work and can respond sensibly and effectively to change: what is frequently lacking is an understanding of what might be termed the 'outer environment', where four major forces of change are at work. These are government activities, technological change, sociological change and economic change—all irresistible forces in their own right and all intertwined with each other (see Figure opposite). The impact of these forces on the outer environment must cause shock waves to the industrial environment and in turn within the firm itself. No organization is or can be insulated.

The marketing auditor, while not losing his introspective approach, must nevertheless remain firmly aware that he operates in a highly volatile environment and can control or influence only a minute proportion of it.

Turning now to the lists themselves, what has been attempted is to devise an extremely wide range of questions covering all the firm's marketing activities and matters pertinent to them. The relevant ones can be selected and, hopefully, from the answers and their relationship with each other will emerge as a series of marketing actions, which will enable a greater exploitation of existing resources to occur. It will indicate resources not required, and which are therefore being wasted, and also resources to be acquired.

Let us take some simple examples. There are, for most firms, about 220 selling days in a year in the UK and 365 in international markets. How many days a year are the salesmen selling, and how is the rest of time accounted for? Is the balance of time spent not in sales situations justified by the cost of the salesman doing something that is either not selling or

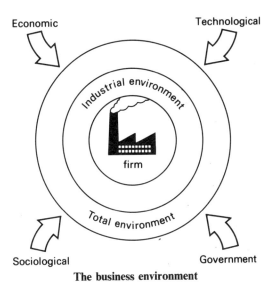

The business environment

not directly relevant to selling, and could it be done as effectively by someone else? How many sales calls are made each week in aggregate and individually? What is the cost per call and what are the time components of that cost, i.e., liaising within the company, preparing quotations, and the many other things a salesman has to do besides the face-to-face sales situation, and which are so often overlooked in any assessment of the salesman's time expenditure. Is one more call per week of average quality possible? With a ten-man sales force and a typical four calls a day striking rate, this represents over 450 additional calls: what is the ratio of enquiries to calls; of quotations to business? Even a highly unfavourable ratio is likely to produce a great deal of extra business. How, then, can that extra call a week be achieved? The answers to these questions, all to be found in List 9, 'The sales force', will rapidly reveal if the sales force is fully productive.

A second example can be drawn from List 11, 'Non-personal promotion: methods and media'. Many firms, but most particularly professional practices and service companies, fail to trace the source of enquiries from new clients or customers, and yet this is the only truly accurate guide as to which messages and which communication techniques are effective. It is very cheap, quick and simple to develop a tracing operation once it is appreciated how much this can contribute to profitable operations by ensuring that all promotion is concentrated on messages and methods that are seen to work.

Finally a glance at List 13, 'The buying process', will draw attention to the fact that all too few salesmen ever look closely into the methods customers use to evaluate products or services or the criteria adopted for judging the end of the useful life of a purchase. This knowledge can sharpen the sales platform to a considerable extent by taking fully into account this key decision factor.

It will be seen that the basic classifications—materials, capital goods, consumer goods, operating supplies, semi-manufacturers and services[1]—have not been separated. The marketing auditor may have to adjust for whatever classification in which he is involved.

In using the lists it may be found that the answers to the questions in the various sections will not be obtainable in one department or from one individual, or even within its firm; therefore it cannot be expected that the audit can be completed in a single session (although

1. Services are a minor exception in that although they are taken into almost every section of the book List 23 *Service Businesses* deals specifically with those aspects of marketing which are peculiar to them.

it is by no means impossible). In my experience it is not usually necessary for each answer, particularly quantitive ones, to be provided with a high degree of precision. A phenomenon or pattern will generally be revealed by reasonable indicators. Precision should be sought only if the resulting action will be affected by the difference between an indicator and the exact position. If a market size is £10 million or £11 million, is it likely to affect the detailed, let alone the basic, marketing strategy?

The order of the lists is in a sense very personal and as such idiosyncratic. Powerful arguments can (and indeed were) made for re-ordering, using a different rationale—the importance of the subject, the sequence within the marketing process, alphabetical, ease of acquiring the data, and so on. The continuum as presented now may appear to lack a formal logic, but it does correspond to a sequence found to work well in an actual audit. It will fit the circumstances of most firms, but if it does not there is no reason whatsoever why the auditor cannot re-order the sequence to his own requirements.

Some questions have been repeated where they are needed in different sections, perhaps for different purposes. Where this occurs the questions have been cross-referenced to save having to re-think the answers. For example, Question 2.23 in the second list, 'Product/service range', on total cost analysis, is repeated in List 20, 'Pricing', as Question 20.29.

Some readers may wonder why there is no section dealing specifically with the marketing message as methods and media are covered at some length. In fact, questions relating to the marketing message with their implications for making it more effective will be found throughout the text: obviously in such Lists as 'The sales force', 'Non-personal promotion: methods and media', 'Product/service range', but perhaps not quite so obviously under the special circumstances of 'Non-differentiated products' and 'Service businesses'.

Each list has a commentary, the purpose of which is to draw attention to some of the key questions and their implications and to illustrate points with short case histories. I have attempted to build into the commentaries a number of suggestions for consideration for action. In List 18, 'Physical distribution', for example, some classic failures are referred to: assuming a punctual despatch date implies a punctual receipt date, and risking blame for late delivery; failure to design a pack that would enable distant, accurate, stock checks to be made by clear marking and 'remaining contents' indicators (where appropriate); failure to use the shipment and storage pack to carry advertising messages. In List 9, 'The sales force', an example is given of how one manufacturer managed to improve his average price obtained by sharing benefits with the salesmen. Many other examples will be found throughout the book.

It is not only markets that are not homogeneous. Customers also are widely varying in their needs, perceptions, policies, and practices. Thus a different answer might well emerge from a number of the questions if they are applied to customers with different profiles. A useful breakdown that can be used as necessary throughout the check lists is:

- Regular customers
- Sporadic customers
- One-off customers
- Lost customers
- Customers inviting quotations but not producing business
- Prospects where no invitation to quote has been obtained

An example of the use of these categorizations will be found in List 16, 'User industries', in the section Introduction and Question 16.11.

Because the attempt has been made to make the subjects covered and the questions as comprehensive as possible, the task of undertaking a marketing audit using the check list approach may look daunting. It need not be so. Typically, an audit for small operations would require less than half of the questions listed. It is difficult to conceive of an occasion when the entire gamut of questions would be needed.

The sectionalization of the lists enables the auditor, if he so wishes, to look at individual parts of the business only, as each list, while cross-referenced, is also free-standing. Thus, if an audit of the agency resources, utilization and methods are required List 10, 'The agency system', can be completed quite independently of any other section.

To obtain the maximum benefit from the compilation the user should see it both as a whole and in its parts.

One final suggestion: the marketing auditor must be totally unbiased and neutral. Internal politics have no part to play in a marketing audit, and management should not expect the auditor to remain objective if he is reporting on a situation that may reflect critically on himself or his department. In selecting a marketing auditor this factor needs careful consideration.

How to use the check lists

It has already been said that the use of the check lists is relatively simple. They require only those skills that most managers would be expected to possess. They do however need a knowledge of the organization and its personnel as well as an ability to obtain co-operation from busy people. This is always best achieved if the purpose of the audit and the outcome is fully explained to those from whom help is sought.

Basically three requirements exist:

- Deciding which questions are relevant
- Knowing where to obtain the information
- Interpreting the answers into terms of actions to be taken

The procedure for use is as follows.

1. First check the documentation required for the audit. Some suggestions for the material that will be needed precedes the first list. Where the requirement for these documents arises will emerge from the lists themselves but again, by way of example, 'Terms of business' referred to in List 4 'Company performance', Questions 4.39–4.41, will obviously need a study of the conditions. If all the documents required could be assembled before the audit begins, much time can be saved.
2. Next, decide which sections can be eliminated. A manufacturer of process plant or *haute couture* fashions will hardly need List 22, 'Non-differentiated products', or a service company List 18, 'Physical distribution'. It is wise however not to assume too readily from the title alone that some of the questions may not be applicable. The fact that a firm does not use distributors does not necessarily imply that there are no questions within the section where the answers may not produce a re-consideration of the policy. It is always better to retain a list if any doubt exists as to its relevance.
3. The requirement now is to prune the remaining lists by deleting all questions that are not applicable or where it is known that the information is just not obtainable. An example of the first situation could come from List 7, 'Market size and structure', Questions 7.29 and 7.30 on in-feeding and reciprocal trading, which will certainly not apply to the general run of companies. Similarly List 20, 'Pricing', Question 20.27: it may simply not be possible to ascertain just what a customer would pay to retain a particular product or service attribute.
4. The auditor will probably find that some questions suggest other questions. While he must certainly not be afraid to add, he should be aware that no check list is ever complete. Every compiler of such lists knows this. New questions always occur, and the lists get longer and longer both as a consequence of change within and external to the company

and because of the answers to the questions themselves. The benefits and dangers of this are too obvious to need spelling out.

5. The main task now starts. The auditor should go through the remaining questions and answer every question that he can do himself and with confidence. It will be found that the ideas for marketing action will emerge from the answers. These ideas should be written down alongside the answers. If this is done in a different colour ink it will enable them to be extracted quickly at a later stage of the audit and grouped according to the classifications required.

In assembling some of the information the auditor may well be able to take a further short-cut by the use of adaptation of some of the excellent formats developed for market planning.[1] A well laid out form can make obtaining and tabulating data much quicker and simpler and thus bring into prominence the action implications.

The reader may also want to refer to the Naylor and Wood[2] approach to marketing audits, which suggests some interesting and useful data analyses as well as some short but highly relevant check lists.

6. This now leaves a number of questions on which the auditor must consult. He should identify those within the organization and, if needs be, outside it which he has to contact. If each question to be administered is marked with respondent's initials or some identification, this will save a great deal of time and indeed some impatience at the time of the actual meeting. If the questions are submitted in writing for preliminary examination, this of course is helpful; but it does involve further loss of time and moreover the loss of spontaneity, particularly on qualitative aspects of the audit, may not off-set the value of the prior consideration. The worst combination is to submit the questions in writing and to ask for a reply in writing: the time delay will be found to be considerable, most particularly when further questions are engendered by the answers or where clarification is needed.

Some points may be better dealt with on a consensus basis, probably using a group of informed personnel with different responsibilities and disciplines. The group approach has the advantage of the Delphi technique, which enables each member to hear the advocacy for and against a particular opinion and if need be to modify his views. However, while suggestions for action should be welcomed, care must be taken not to get into a stultifying position of arguing about theory. It is the job of the auditor to decide what the implications of the information are. An action plan by a committee is going to be the antithesis of quick movement and decisiveness.

Some recycling of both answers and action recommendations may well be needed, and the auditor should be prepared for these and be able to accommodate them. The best results will ensue if no firm attitudes are taken or decisions adopted until all the answers are in and all the actions summarized.

7. It is recognized that not everything can be done within the resources and time span available, so it may be necessary to place an order of priority on the introduction of changes or activities that are deemed necessary. To this end it is advisable to extract all action points for categorization into priority groups with an indication of, at the very least, the time implied by such terms as 'at once', 'short-term', 'medium-term', and 'long-term'. On their own, time designations of this type have no real meaning.

It would also be useful to classify by likely cost implications, so that no-cost and low-cost items can be proceeded with without budget changes or authorization. This alone should ensure the removal of one possible blockage.

1. John Stapleton, *How to Prepare a Marketing Plan*, Gower Press, Epping, 1974.
2. John Naylor and Alan Wood, *Practical Marketing Audits*, Associated Business Programmes, London, 1978.

8. The last action of the audit is to place a date for initiation and completion of each activity, to decide who is responsible for carrying it through and who is to be responsible for monitoring progress and satisfactory completion.

The audit process can now be summarized.

- Collect documentation
- Eliminate all non-applicable sections
- Delete all non-relevant questions in the remaining sections
- Answer all questions within the capability of the auditor, with recommended courses of action
- List others who need to be consulted to complete audit
- Decide whether to take individual replies or operate as a group
- (for individual responses) Identify which questions will be asked of which persons
- (for individual responses) Decide how response will be taken; i.e., personal interview, advance notice of questions and personal interview, written request and written response
- Write in the suggested courses of action arising from the responses
- Extract all action points and categorize according to urgency, likely cost, ease of implementation, etc.
- Allocate each task by name, schedule it by date or elapsed time, agree monitoring procedure

The last point requires extra emphasis. Completing an audit does not automatically imply that the appropriate actions will be taken. To be certain that the marketing resources will be fully realized, it is important to ensure that every action decided is allocated to an individual or group, that the time for its completion is scheduled and promulgated and that someone has the task of monitoring that the task is satisfactorily completed by the due date. *Allocate*, *schedule* and *monitor* are the key words for guaranteeing action.

The marketing audit is *not* a substitute for action, nor should it be permitted to delay decision-taking. This is a thought that the auditor should keep foremost in his mind when undertaking the audit.

Documentation

The internal marketing audit will be considerably assisted, and much time will be saved, if the appropriate documentation is collected or made available before the audit begins. Users of the list are advised to obtain as many of the following documents as appropriate; where the volume of paper is considerable, as in the case of enquiry and sales records, access to them should be cleared with the appropriate managers. The lack of any of these data may well indicate an information gap to be filled.

- Organization chart (official and informal)
- Corporate/market/profit plan
- Catalogues and brochures (own and competitors')
- Media advertising and direct mail material (including schedules) and appropriations
- Salesmen's reporting form
- Enquiry records
- Sales analyses
- Salesmen's, agents' and distributors' assessment forms
- New product search report and evaluations
- List of journals, etc., received
- List of external statistics received regularly
- Guarantee claim record
- Service records
- Agency agreement forms
- Terms of business

This is a documentation requirement for a typical audit. There will be other data needed, as will be seen from the check lists, and of course each company will have specific requirements. The use of the documents will become obvious as the audit proceeds.

List 1.   Marketing strategy and planning

Introduction

The first check list deals with the fundamental activities involved in creating a marketing strategy and implementing it. Strategies and plans should always be available to all managers, not just those involved in marketing. They do not have to be formal and complex, but they should always be in a written form.

The plan ought to give the assumptions on which it is based, the resources available for its implementation, a conceptualization of the market position and potential, forecasts—technical, commercial, economic, financial, and specific to the firm—threats and opportunities, courses of action and activity schedule, personnel plan, budgets, controls, and monitoring. Question 1.1 implies all this, while Question 1.5 focuses in on the all-important subject of objectives.

It is important at the outset to check that objectives do indeed exist and are understood, that they are practical, and also that they are acceptable to those who must achieve them. It has to be seen by everyone involved that goals are compatible with the market potential and the company resources. Setting out objectives may also give a good indication of the strategies and tactics to be adopted.

This first list is designed to ensure that elegant plans are not just documents for perusing. They must have action points built in, with both monitoring and fail-safe facilities.

Question 1.7 on gap analysis refers to the simple technique of making a surprise free forecast of sales in the next five years—usually a straight line (momentum) projection—and comparing the position of the graph in the fifth year with the quantitive targets (see Fig. 1-1). Any shortfall, which is the gap between the projection and the target set, represents the task that marketing must accomplish, which in turn will demonstrate how realistic the targets are.

Question 1.17 calls for a segmentation of the market. Segmentation is a vital technique in marketing, and failure to distinguish the parts from the whole can lead to massive under-performance. Few markets are wholly homogeneous. Identifying segments with common characteristics that will cause them to respond to the same marketing messages and marketing tools as other segments will enable the firm to concentrate its marketing resources in the most effective way.

There are many ways of segmenting a market. Some obvious ones are: by region, size of customer company, form of customer organization, heavy or light users, seasonal, demographic factors, psychographic factors and, a particularly interesting and useful one, by benefit received.

Appendix 1A gives a model of this last method for a variable chamber filter. Industries appearing under the *primary impact sector* heading in the left-hand column only are

2

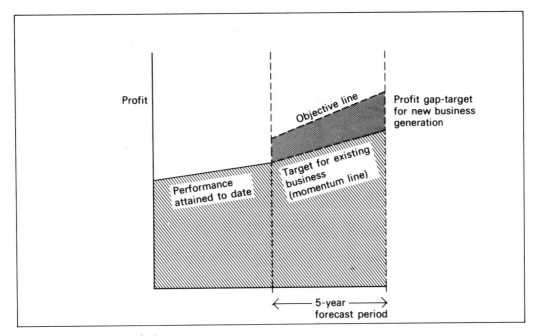

Figure 1-1 The gap analysis

obviously more likely to view the product favourably than those in the right-hand column. The segmentation priority is obvious. For firms appearing in both central columns it is necessary to judge how far the disadvantages of the filter for their processes offset the advantages, and to decide the balance.

It is important to start the audit with an understanding of the perceived strengths and weaknesses of the firm as well as of its opportunities and the threats to which it is exposed. The audit as it proceeds may cause a radical review of any profile, but this first assessment will give a useful benchmark. It will also reveal how much of the profile is based on in-company folklore and how much on the real situation. Question 1.21 deals with this key issue. Answers might well be obtained by the use of a simple form distributed to key personnel (not just necessarily managers) and a consensus of the views taken on the major issues.

This type of analysis is known by its acronym SOFT (*S*trength *O*pportunity *F*ault *T*hreat). The suggested content is shown in Fig. 1-2.[1]

Perhaps a new thought to many marketing men will be Question 1.23 on marketing vulnerability. Vulnerability analysis substitutes a precise and disciplined methodology for emotional or even hysterical reactions to emerging threats or, at the opposite extreme, a 'don't let's look, it might go away' philosophy.

The technique was first developed by Stanford Research Institute and has put a new discipline into contingency planning by devising a formal methodology. It is necessary first to identify the underpinnings of the business—that is, the critical factors for successful operation—and then to formulate any threats that may destroy the underpinnings. Selected individuals are then invited to consider each threat and to give their personal judgement on

1. E. P. Learned, C. R. Christensen, K. R. Andrews, and W. D. Guth, *Business Policy—Texts and Cases*, Irwin, Homewood, Ill., 1969, pp. 175–83; and *Planning a Diversification Strategy*, Industrial Market Research Ltd, London, 1979, p. 7.

```
                        SOFT Analysis
              (Please use one form for each point raised)


        THE FOLLOWING IS ONE POINT IN OUR COMPANY'S FUTURE


   1. Name _____        Job Title_____


   2. This issue refers to a: (tick one only)
                        Strength  ☐         Opportunity ☐
                        Fault     ☐         Threat      ☐
        in our (tick one only)
                        Company   ☐
                        Suppliers ☐
                        Customers ☐


   3. Description or statement of point


   4. References, sources or facts


   5. Range of possible action or resource requirements
```

Figure 1-2

its likely impact and the chance of its occurring. A consensus is then taken of each threat by grouping on to one matrix the judgements of the individuals involved in the exercise. If there are wide disparities of views, each person is invited to give the basis for the position he has allotted the threat, and, through re-cycling, a Delphi forecast is produced.

The same grid is used both for the individual personal assessments and the consensus results (see Fig. 1-3).

Any grouping substantially in the top right-hand quartile requires immediate avoiding action, while the top left and bottom right quartiles call for monitoring and a contingency plan to ensure that the threats do not move up or across into the top right-hand quartile.[1]

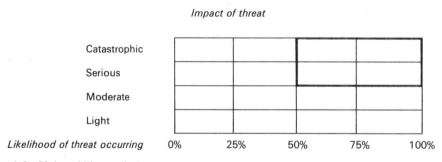

Figure 1-3 Vulnerability analysis

1. Douglas A. Hurd, *Vulnerability Analysis in Business Planning*, SRI, Menlo Park, Calif., 1977.

4

With hindsight, it might have been foreseen that the demand for cheap cassette recorders and tapes had a high probability of developing the severe effect that commercial record companies are now experiencing. Will this be repeated with video and the commercial cinema?

Vulnerability analysis is a simple exercise once the underpinnings of the business are agreed and an ordered approach to the consideration of threats is substituted for hysteria or complacency.

Product planning is a vital part of marketing strategy, although it is sometimes seen, wrongly, as completely separate. Question 1.28 asks pertinent questions of how a range is composed, and the implication of specialization and full-line trading is inherent.

In small companies, devising a marketing strategy and planning its implementation can be relatively quick and simple. In the larger firms more discipline is required. However, these activities can easily evolve into tasks in their own right. It is a good rule that planning should never become such a burden that it distracts from and interferes with the day-to-day running of the company. This must not happen. It need not happen if a realistic view is taken of what planning can and should be done. The first check list is basic but helps identify the many issues involved.

1.1 Do we have a formal forward marketing plan?

1.2 Is it compatible with other operational and project plans?

1.3 What period is covered?

1.4 When was it last reviewed and revised?

1.5 Do we have agreed quantitative and qualitative objectives?
- Profit
- Value of sales
- Unit sales
- Number of customers
- Market share
- Market penetration
- Return on investment
- New products
- Range coverage
- Geographical coverage

1.6 Are the objectives reviewed regularly as to their relevance?

1.7 Have we conducted a gap analysis to appraise the nature of the marketing task and the resource requirement and if so how large is the gap? (See Introduction.)

1.8 Will the market plan, if carried out successfully, close the gap?

1.9 What resources will be needed to close the gap and will they be made available?

1.10 Is there a marketing plan, by product/service?

1.11 Do all or relevant managers have copies of the marketing plan?

1.12 How and when is the marketing plan regularly used by managers?

1.13 Are individual market tasks defined and allocated, and scheduled, and is accomplishment monitored?

1.14 Who is responsible for these tasks, i.e., allocating, scheduling, and monitoring?

1.15 What methods exist for dealing with non-completion or unsatisfactory completion of allocated tasks?

1.16 Is there a contingency plan against failed targets?

1.17 Are market segments defined in an order of priority? (See Introduction and some suggested criteria in List 2, 'Product/service range', Question 2.2 and List 16, 'User industries', Question 16.9.)

1.18 What criteria were adopted to identify the segment priorities?

1.19 Are they still valid?

1.20 Does the allocation of marketing resources reflect the segment priorities? (See Introduction and List 11, 'Non-personal promotion: methods and media'.)

1.21 Have we made an analysis of the company strengths, weaknesses, opportunities, and threats? (See List 4, 'Company performance', Question 4.1.)

1.22 Does the product/service and communication 'mix' reflect the strength profile?

1.23 Have we identified major vulnerabilities, their impact, and the likelihood of occurring? (See Introduction and List 7, 'Market size and structure', Questions 7.18–7.20 and List 8, 'Future market', Introduction.)

1.24 Do we have a contingency plan for dealing with threats?

1.25 What actions have been taken to mitigate corporate weaknesses?

1.26 Has the SOFT analysis revealed any unexploited opportunities? (See Introduction.)

1.27 What actions are proposed to utilize these?

1.28 Have we a product/service plan?

1.29 Does it include range 'mix', range 'depth', range 'width' additions and deletions? (See Introduction.)

1.30 Are the three elements of strategy—segmentation, marketing 'mix', and product planning—all compatible?

Appendix 1A. Segmentation by benefit received

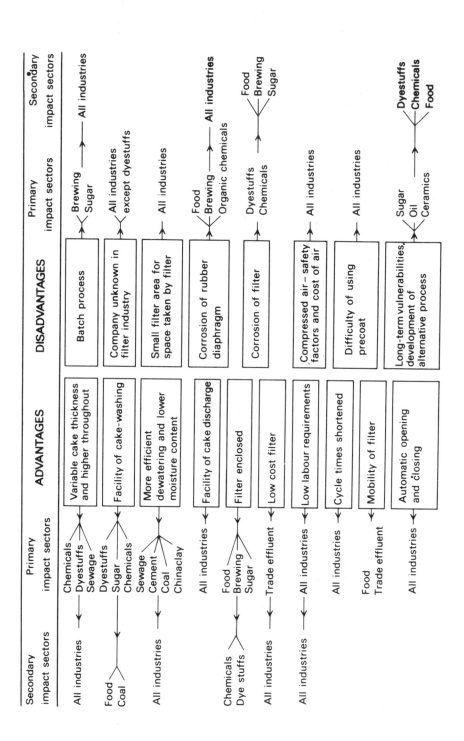

List 2. Product/service range

Introduction

This second list now brings us to the product or service to be marketed. It is appreciated that Question 2.2 could open up a huge field of enquiry for even the smallest firms. The marketing auditor, in undertaking or instructing analysis, must decide what is applicable and what is merely interesting. The question suggests some typical and relevant headings, but the auditor must decide which to use and any other that will throw light on the range performance.

Apart from sales analysis, there are other useful indicators, such as ratio, correlation and actuarial analyses, which can yield valuable information on both the market and competitors from the firm's own records.[1]

Question 2.3 is a sign-post to indicate a common marketing trap. Low sellers may be viewed as unprofitable in terms of production runs, inventory, and sales efforts, but the question seeks an answer as to whether the low sellers in fact have a marketing function far more valuable than the sales they achieve: that is, do the low sellers make a marketing contribution in a perceptual sense in that they assist the sales of the other products? Do they add credibility to the company as specialists within a product group or range; do they attract business for other products/services?

Indirect marketing is an important and frequently neglected function. This is a situation where others outside the purchasing organization may have a strong or total influence over any purchase. Typical of such indirect marketing targets are standards institutions, trade associations, governmental and para-statal bodies, and consultants. These are as much a legitimate marketing target as the actual buying organization itself. Questions 2.10, 2.11, and 2.19–2.22 draw attention to this situation.

Question 2.23 is of particular interest and comes up again in the same or different forms in several other places in the lists. All too often a product or service is simply quoted on the basis of what the customer pays. But the real price of a product or service may be far higher than the amount at the bottom of an invoice. Asking what a product really costs is important. List 20, 'Pricing', gives an example in Fig. 20-1 of a 'true-price' model, where the real and hidden costs of two comparable products are demonstrated to a customer. This can often swing the buyer to the apparently higher priced offer when the totality of costs is known.

Question 2.27 brings in for the first time the question of 'benefits'. Selling benefits is now part of the standard approach of most firms but it is more honoured in its breach than its observance. Moreover, customers are now more sophisticated in their purchasing pro-

1. Aubrey Wilson, *The Assessment of Industrial Markets*, Associated Business Programmes, London, 1973, Chapter 5.

cedures, and it has become increasingly necessary to *prove* that benefits will in fact be received.

The test as to whether the company is really marketing benefits is easily made. Take the company catalogue or brochure and underline in one colour every feature mentioned. Underline in another colour every benefit the customer obtains. For most firms the number of features far outweighs the benefits, and yet customers buy the product only for what it will do for them, not for what it is: that merely provides the proof or otherwise that he will receive the benefits. High speed to the customer may equal increased output; heavy gauge may equal safety; modularity may equal flexibility. Thus customers buy output, safety, and flexibility—not speed, gauge, or modularity. The fundamental question to which attention must be given is, 'Do we sell what our customers buy?'

Completion of the model in Fig. 2-1 for each product will provide excellent guidance for the promotional and personal selling platform.

New product/service introductions are dealt with in List 15.

Product/service _____

FEATURES The facts about our product, service, company, system, etc.	FUNCTIONS How it works Why it works How it is used	BENEFITS What does this mean to him? Be specific	PROOF How can you prove that he will receive the benefit?	QUESTIONS Does he need the benefit? Does he want it? (Leading)

Figure 2-1 A model for personal selling and promotional platform

Question 2.42 draws attention to the old but nevertheless valid marketing approach of developing something unique in the product/service or in the cluster of surrounding benefits. Of course, a patentable innovation can achieve a USP (Unique Selling Proposition), although it is increasingly difficult to hold a patent lead for any length of time, and in any event services are not patentable. For most companies it is usually better to seek to develop a collection of benefits which on their own would not be unique but as a package offer a distinctly perceivable 'plus'. While it is also true that these advantages cannot be held for long, being first does have distinct benefits. An example can be taken from a service industry—banking. With a market target of, say, farmers, a USP might comprise the following:

- Wide experience of small business enterprises
- Understanding of and contact with commodity market
- Knowledge of farmers' financial problems and needs
- Close involvement in community affairs and local business
- Loan products geared to seasonal and climatic factors

An examination of product features and performance as well as of supporting services linked to customer needs and problems can without difficulty establish practical USPs.

Information on the perceived and actual useful life of a product, particularly if it is compared with customers experience and views on competitor products, can give valuable product and marketing insights. The technique of actuarial analysis (probabilities of life expectancies) is a useful internal analysis tool substantially achieved by the study of service records. Question 2.45 looks into this often neglected aspect of marketing and customer relations.

2.1 List product/service ranges, including quality spread.

2.2 Analyse sales by each characteristic, application, and market segment (See Introduction):

Geographical

Process or application

Frequency of purchase

Benefit received

Form of customer organization

Demographic factors

Lead time required

Buyer's job function

Guarantee claims

Cost per sale

Reason for purchase

Industry or trade

Credit requirements

Size of order

Size of customer operation

Psychographic factors

Full line or limited purchase

Seasonal

Servicing requirements

Order source (e.g. OEM distributor)

Value added

(Some of this information will be required again in List 7, 'Market size and structure', Question 7.10, and the items are repeated in List 16, 'User industries', Question 16.9.)

2.3 What justification is there for keeping low sales items in range? (See Introduction.)

2.4 How many and which products are own developments? How many licensed? How many traded? How many franchised? How much sub-contract work? (This answer will be required again in List 15, 'Introducing new products/services', Questions 15.1 and 15.25, and should also be compared with List 4, 'Company performance', Question 4.16.)

2.5 Is this 'mix' satisfactory?

2.6 If not, what steps can we take to adjust closer to a desideratum?

2.7 List major and subsidiary uses for the products/services. (See Introduction to List 7, 'Market size and structure', and Questions 7.5–7.9.)

2.8 Do existing customers know our full range and the major and subsidiary uses for the products/services?

2.9 Are our products incorporated into any other products?

2.10 Do they require, or would sales be assisted by, OEM approval for incorporation?

2.11 If we do not have all OEM approvals, what steps do we take to obtain them?

2.12 Are our products identifiable as our make when incorporated into users' product or otherwise processed?

2.13 If not, can they be?

2.14 What is the form of identification? Can it be made irremovable?

2.15 Do any of the products carry customers' or other private brands? If so, which?

2.16 What is the justification for accepting private branding? Is it still valid?

2.17 Are there any British, American, or European standards to which the products/services must conform?

2.18 If not, can they be referenced to as 'above' a known standard? (See answers in List 22, 'Non-differentiated products', Questions 22.9–22.15.)

2.19 What degree of control over specifications do customers, end customers, consultants, or contractors exercise? (See List 5, 'Export marketing', Question 5.42, List 7, 'Market size and structure', Question 7.32, and List 13, 'The buying process', Question 13.2.)

2.20 How do they exercise it?

2.21 Have we identified any other influences over specifications that should be considered (e.g., government, insurance companies, financial institutions, etc.)?

2.22 What steps have we taken to initiate and maintain contact with these influences?

2.23 Do products/services have any total cost effectiveness advantages over directly or indirectly competitive products/services? (See Introduction to List 20, 'Pricing', and particularly Fig. 20-1; Introduction to List 17, 'Competitive climate', Question 17.59; and List 22, 'Non-differentiated products', Questions 22.33–22.35.)

2.24 Does our promotion emphasize this?

2.25 Can we undertake a cost effectiveness exercise for the customer?

2.26 What are the principle features of our products/services?

2.27 Have we translated these into benefits, as seen by purchasers? (See Fig. 2-1, and the answer should also be considered with those in List 13, 'The buying process', Questions 13.10, 13.17, and 13.20; and List 14, 'Analysing lost business', Question 14.9.)

2.28 Does our sales and promotional platform emphasize these benefits? (This answer is required again in List 9, 'The sales force', Question 9.43; List 11, 'Non-personal promotion: methods and media', Question 11.33; and in a somewhat different form in List 20, 'Pricing', Question 20.30.)

2.29 What are the products/services deficiencies?

2.30 If they are not irradicable, what trade-off does the customer get?

2.31 What support do other products/services provided give the main products/services range (e.g., extends range, production or procurement advantages, selling to same buyers)? (See List 3, 'The service element in marketing'.)

2.32 Do any of our competitors specialize?

2.33 How does our own policy differ in this respect?

2.34 What is the reason for our respective policies?

2.35 Do we need to reconsider ours in the light of competitors' performances and their image?

2.36 What have been the major technological changes over the past five years in the product/service group?

2.37 Do our products/services incorporate these changes?

2.38 What percentage of our business is 'specials' and what percentage 'standards'?

2.39 Do we want to shift the balance?

2.40 Does our marketing plan allow for any change in range spread?

2.41 Do we have any knowledge of the product/service life cycle?

2.42 Do we have or can we develop some unique aspect in our offering which will differentiate us favourably from competitors? (See Introduction and List 11, 'Non-personal promotion: methods and media', Question 11.34.)

2.43 Can we draw a profile of an 'ideal' product/service from the viewpoint of each major user segment? (This information will be needed to answer List 17, 'Competitive climate', Question 17.50.)

2.44 Can we list the factors that prevent us from developing our offer closer to the 'ideal'?

2.45 What criteria are used to judge the end of the useful life of the product and are they the same as those applied to competitors products? (This question comes up a number of times and the answer will be required for List 13, 'The buying process', Question 13.39; List 16, 'User industries', Question 16.43; List 17, 'Competitive climate', Question 17.53; and List 20, 'Pricing', Question 20.21.)

List 3.   The service element in marketing

Introduction

This section of the marketing audit check list concerns itself with back-up services (as distinct from services marketed in their own right as profit centres dealt with in List 23, 'Service businesses') that are either vital or desirable. In many instances quality and reliability of the service element distinguishes otherwise indistinguishable products. With products made to a standard, the marketing response tends to be on price. This is usually as wrong as it is unnecessary. Theodore Levitt refers to surrounding the product with a cluster of customer-satisfying benefits, many of which will be services, as a way of distinguishing one offering from another. A prime example of this was found in Australia, where one supplier of ready-mix concrete, a classical non-differentiated product, not only dominated a highly competitive market but did so at a marginally higher price than its competitors. The secret was the supplier's reputation for punctuality in site delivery and the employment of co-operative drivers who would drop the load at precisely the point the site foreman required. The premium price was considered justified by the reduction of site problems and the improvement in labour relations. (The subject of differentiating otherwise non-distinguishable products is dealt with fully in List 22, 'Non-differentiated products'.)

Of course, a question to be considered is whether a firm should undertake any or all of the service requirements. Sub-contracting is an option worth considering. Question 3.11 raises this point early on in looking at the whole complex that comprises service back-up in a company.

Services that support the product can be of three types: profit-making in their own right, cost-recovering, and not charged. 'Free' is a misnomer; there is, as has been frequently pointed out, no such thing as a free lunch. The cost of service in the last category is part of the purchase price. List 2, 'Product/service range', Question 2.23 touches on this point. Many firms give away services that can be sold profitably and, equally, lose sales because the cost of service or spares is seen by customers as unrealistically high. The attitude of British domestic equipment suppliers in attempting to sell service contracts is to be compared with Miele, the German firm, whose policy can be described as 'send for us only when you need us'. The latter says something about the quality of their equipment, while the former, however much it may be justified commercially, is psychologically damaging. The check list attempts to force a consideration of these and other aspects of service.

Because there will be frequent reference throughout the lists to the service back-up, the various services that are referred to in the following section have been encapsulated in Appendix 3A for quick reference.

The first question is of great importance, since companies frequently overlook important services and maintain services that are either not of real value or could more efficiently be conducted by the customer. Some services are identified but they are generalized, and each firm should consider specific services related to its product. Which services shall be provided and the financial basis to be adopted is a key decision. If the attitude of the company is that services are an unfortunate necessity, then the line of thinking must be towards developing the product to reduce service or make servicing simple and economic for the customer to undertake (e.g., plug-in replacement units).

A firm of manufacturers of reverse jet filters, in considering this point and the problem of servicing distant customers, re-designed the method of removing the filter elements so that it could be done in less than half the time required for conventional filters and at the same time gave more headroom for the work to be carried out. These improvements enabled the customers to use unskilled and thus lower-cost labour for the maintenance, and saved the service charges. The modification was a powerful selling tool.

Improved works manuals, and indeed multi-channel programmed tape instruction systems, can completely change the nature of servicing and the demand on service requirements from the supply firms.

The marketing auditor must not however confuse 'services' with 'servicing'. As the list demonstrated, not all services are by any means related to servicing equipment. Services should be viewed in the widest sense and not thought of as substantially technical matters.

Question 3.13 may highlight missed prospects. The service engineer could well be the first person to see a sales opening, since he has access to customer plant or equipment. Obviously he should be encouraged in some tangible way to report back on such opportunities.

Question 3.15 draws attention to the advantages to be gained from sales and service staff working closely together. It is the practice of one engineering company to ensure that salesmen make at least occasional service calls with the service engineers and that they in turn make sales calls with the salesmen. Obtaining an insight into each other's problems, working environment, and situation has been found invaluable in producing a synergy that has measurable results in sales.

It should also not be forgotten that the service engineer is likely to be the member of the company seen most frequently by the customer, and his reliability, punctuality, skill, and manner will have an all-pervading effect on the company's image.

Many firms can provide service back-up if requested but fail to see that the availability of these services can influence both the business obtained and good customer relations. It should be axiomatic that if services exist they should be promoted. Question 3.34 covers this point.

3.1 What back-up services do we provide? (Use Questions 3.16, 3.21, 3.24, 3.25, 3.27, 3.28, 3.29, 3.33, and 3.37 as a guide to possible services which could be offered, but see Appendix 3A for more detail.)

3.2 What criteria have been used for deciding whether to adopt or reject them? Are they still valid?

3.3 Which services are profit-making, which cost-recovering, and which not charged?

3.4 What information do we have on customer attitudes to each service and charge method?

3.5 Would the values that customers place on any service justify its being re-classified? (See Question 3.3 above and the Introduction to List 20, 'Pricing', on 'Price and the Perception of Performance'.)

3.6 What is customer attitude to provision of services?

3.7 What is our attitude to the provision of services? Should it be changed?

3.8 What is our customers' view on the quality and reliability of our services?

3.9 Is our service staff adequate in number and skills?

3.10 Do service staff appreciate their importance in projecting the image of the company? (See List 21, 'Images and perceptions'.)

3.11 Should we consider sub-contracting some or all services to an outside organization?

3.12 Can any deficiency in service staff be remedied by training and re-motivation?

3.13 Is the service staff integrated into mainstream company activity?

3.14 Are service engineers and other staff motivated to seek opportunities for sales?

3.15 What liaison is there between service staff and marketing?

3.16 How quickly can our emergency services be activated? (See Appendix 3A.)

3.17 Does our sales and promotional platform give this information?

3.18 What would it cost to shorten an emergency response?

3.19 Are the arrangements for customers calling in emergency services satisfactory to them (e.g., office hours only, 24-hour manned telephone service, answering machine)?

3.20 Would the cost of an improved emergency service either be recoverable or would it significantly assist further sales and improve customer relations?

3.21 What design services are required? (See Appendix 3A.)

3.22 Do our design staff have sufficient opportunity to meet customers and to understand their problems and aspirations?

3.23 Would it be a useful extension of services to retain freelance or independent consultants to augment the design team for design functions we cannot at present fulfil?

3.24 What pre-start-up services are required? (See Appendix 3A.)

3.25 What negotiation services are required? (See Appendix 3A.)

3.26 Are customer complaints monitored to establish (a) if a pattern exists; (b) how customer problems are progressed through the company; (c) the extent of customer satisfaction/dissatisfaction after completion of service; (d) the cost of guarantee claims? (On guarantee claims see Introduction to List 11, 'Non-personal promotion: methods and media'. Cost details will be called for in List 20, and List 24, 'Product/service financial information', Question 24.41.)

3.27 What education services are required? (See Appendix 3A and List 19, 'Industry contacts', Question 19.27.)

3.28 What visiting services are required? (See Appendix 3A.)

3.29 What maintenance and repair services are required? (See Appendix 3A.)

3.30 Can we modify the product to reduce the number of visits required?

3.31 Can we improve our works manuals and instruction methods to enable customers to cut service costs?

3.32 What product adaptation services are required? (See Appendix 3A.)

3.33 What stand-by facilities for emergency and peak load periods are required? (See Appendix 3A.)

3.34 What operating services such as consumable supplies and waste disposal are required? (See Appendix 3A.)

3.35 What delivery services are needed? (See Appendix 3A and List 18, 'Physical distribution'.)

3.36 Would a marketing support service be valued by the customer, e.g., joint promotion? (See Appendix 3A.)

3.37 Are there any financial services customers require and would appreciate? (See Appendix 3A.)

3.38 If we volunteered any of the services listed rather than reacted to a request, would it lead to better customer relations and more business?

3.39 Do service personnel provide full details of visits?

3.40 Is it possible to extract market information, general and specific, from such reports? (See List 6, 'Marketing information: systems and use', Question 6.9.)

3.41 Does marketing management receive service personnel reports?

3.42 What operating services are required? (See Appendix 3A.)

3.43 What delivery services are needed? (See Appendix 3A.)

Appendix 3A. Summary of services that can comprise part of a firm's product/service back-up

1. *Design services*
   Physical planning
   Pre-sale service and advice
   Prototype fabrication
   Equipment design and checking
   Facilities advice
   Packaging advice

2. *Pre-start-up services*
   Assembly
   Installation
   Engineering and inspection and testing

3. *Negotiation services*
   Resolving complaints
   Warranty adjustments, including exchange of product
   Liaison between customers and production department

4. *Education services*
   Guidance on application, use, and adaptation of products to customers' needs
   On-site demonstration, instructions, training, and in-plant lectures
   Handling and safety advice
   Library service
   Technical literature
   General industrial advice

5. *Visiting services*
   General and specific-purpose visits to customers' plants
   Customer visits to service and production departments

6. *Maintenance and repair services*
   Periodic testing and adjustment
   Cleaning and repairing
   Rehabilitation and reconditioning
   Loan equipment availability

7. *Product adaptation services*
   Modifications
   Applications research

8. *Emergency services*

9. *Standby services*

10. *Operating services*
    Consumables supplies and stocks
    Waste and packing disposal

11. *Delivery services*
    Stocks
    Van sales
    Rack jobbing
    Consignment (sale or return)

12. *Marketing services*
    Joint promotions
    New product or application development
    Merchandizing aids

13. *Financial services*
    Credit
    Lease, rent or hire
    Buy-back or trade-in
    Factoring
    Discounting

List 4. Company performance

Introduction

This next list provides an important benchmark, since it is concerned with past and present performance against which must be measured the success of any future marketing efforts. The analyses that are suggested should identify strengths and weaknesses and give a clear direction to changes that are needed.

Company performance, more than any other part of the audit, can be subjected to the most varied, complex, and detailed scrutiny. There is a considerable danger of the whole audit getting bogged down at this stage. The questions given below should be regarded as a framework subject to deletion and substitution. The marketing auditor must consider what other aspects of the company performance are relevant and must be taken into account if they impact on the marketing performance. For example, there are no questions on staff numbers, quality, recruitment, turnover—vital in a service organization where, typically, 'people' costs represents 70–80 per cent of total operating costs, while the remainder are substantially 'people'-related, e.g., occupational costs, insurance, office supplies.

Many of the points for consideration are subjected to further questioning in later lists. Again by way of example, this section calls for a look at advertising expenditure but asks nothing about its effectiveness, which will emerge in List 11, 'Non-personal promotion: methods and media'.

The types of vulnerabilities that the analysis may well bring out is a heavy dependence on a few customers; industries or applications that are themselves highly vulnerable to the vicissitudes of an increasingly interdependent international industrial economy; technological change, government intervention, or sociological adjustment—all referred to in the Introduction to the book and in the figure on page xiii.

Even new technologies may find themselves under attack. Is the new information technology already impacting on the demand for computer typesetting, and are some businesses heavily dependent on this sector of the computer business? The call is clearly to look not just at the performance as shown by the data, but at the explanations also. From this will emerge the course of action to adopt.

The market segmentations referred to in the Introduction of List 1, 'Marketing strategy and planning', and specifically in Question 1.17, are now subject to analysis. Questions 4.4, 4.5, and 4.8–4.11 all look at the performance relative to the segments. In the case of Question 4.10, it will often be found that an apparently satisfactory figure disguises hidden potential in some areas. For example, a multi-industry or multi-application material may have a creditable performance in one segment—say, disposable work wear—but it may well not be achieving a satisfactory penetration in another segment—say, labels and packaging use.

Appendix 4A gives a format for analysis; even if the regional market sizes, user industries or applications are not known, it is often possible to complete the columns such as 'number of potential accounts', which may give at least a simplistic view as to whether market coverage matches up to apparent potential.

Questions 4.12 and 4.14 have interesting and practical implications. Relatively few companies examine the impact of a different sales 'mix' in their product range and order size. Although small orders are usually regarded as less profitable, this is frequently a piece of industrial folklore that has little basis in fact. An 'ideal' product/service range and order size mix takes into account not only the economies of scale and procurement, machine and skill loading, but also sales costs. A small order obtained from one department of a customer where other departments are also ordering goods or services may well be significantly more profitable than a larger order from a firm purchasing only one product or service. The permutations are many. These enquiries open the door for a new look at the firm's performance based on the current 'mix' and an ideal 'mix' to be designated.

The product life-cycle, which is referred to in List 2, 'Product/service range', is important in relation to Questions 4.16 and 4.17. Reference back to the answer to Question 2.4 on sources of new product ideas and 2.41 on life-cycles should be cross-referenced with the replies to Questions 4.16 and 4.17.

The rate of new product/service introductions must vary from company to company, but certainly, whatever the periodicity is, there ought to be a rhythm. The moment for feeding in a new product (or extending the life-cycle of an existing one) is at some point before the growth curve plateaus ('top-out'). Unfortunately, identifying 'top-out' conditions is not easy because of managers' reluctance to believe that a product on which they have lavished much love and care, and may well have staked some element of their progress in the company, is suffering with a terminal disease. A plateau is often disguised as a col with swelling up-hills of continued growth beyond. This is a dangerous delusion. The warning signs of 'top-out' can sometimes be defined before a product is even introduced. Even if this is not possible, the marketing auditor should at the very least be sensitive to any phenomenon that might indicate the need to feed in a new product. List 15, 'Introducing new products/services', will cover this subject in more depth.

The section on distributors is also expanded considerably in List 12, 'The distributive system'. The questions here refer only to the distributors in relation to the company's performance.

Questions 4.34 and 4.38 touch on the only two absolutes in marketing. The first is that a firm must be known to exist before buying action can occur. Question 4.34 relates to this 'visibility' and refers to the extent to which the company is known either with aided or unaided recall among customers and potential customers. Obtaining visibility is the first vital stage in the communication process, obtaining an understanding of the message (comprehension) and belief in the claims (conviction) being the other two steps preceding a favourable buying decision. List 11, 'Non-personal promotion: methods and media', gives a model in Fig. 11-1, which illustrates the communication process. All firms should satisfy themselves that they are 'visible' to those who might influence a purchase.

Question 4.38 opens up an equally vital area. The second absolute in marketing is that there has to be a reason why customers prefer one firm to another. This reason may be trivial or fundamental, but it exists. Whatever the reason, it is a strength to be promoted to all customers of the same type. Every firm, without exception, has a differentiated advantage, but very few firms consciously or consistently search for this nugget, and even fewer exploit it when they find it. The implication of the answers to these last two questions will be obvious enough to the marketing auditor.

It is important to trace the source of all enquiries, since this is the one certain way of knowing which methods of promotion are working. 'Working' in this context has a number of meanings. Question 4.35 requires the examination of a particularly bad omission in many firms' marketing operations. If direct mail, for example, raises enquiries but there is a low conversion rate to business as against exhibitions, which raise few enquiries but a great deal of business, it indicates that the former may be good for 'visibility' but that somewhere along the line interest is lost. This in turn could cause an examination of the communication method, the media, or perhaps the message in that initial expectations of potential customers are not fulfilled. A system that identifies how enquiries and business originate is an extremely low-cost activity to introduce and has a value far outweighing the time and effort involved. The analyses have a great number of uses, as will be obvious throughout these lists.

The final questions are a very frequently overlooked aspect of the firm's operations and have some impact on its image. However much a company may seek to project 'nice people to deal with' image, dictatorial pronouncements, even in tiny faint print on the back of the order confirmations, can do considerable damage. Varying from announcing that the company is not responsible for late delivery (who is, then?) to the statement that the contract shall be interpreted under British law, the clauses are often as anachronistic as they are unreal.

That they are unreal is illustrated by the fact that few companies either choose or want to litigate with their customers, and while the stated conditions of business might give them a strong legal case, if they will not be used they serve no purpose and are counter-productive in a marketing sense.

By way of example, no single instance comes to mind of a consulting company in the marketing or management field ever suing a client for premature termination of a contract; yet many consultants' terms of business specify that under such circumstances the full fee becomes payable. These firms are well aware that publicization of such litigation would do them considerable harm. They make a virtue of necessity and offer premature termination without penalty, charging fees incurred to date.

If contract terms are written by lawyers, it is not surprising they are restrictive and comprise what is hoped (but rarely proves to be) an unanswerable case in a situation that is never going to go into court anyway. All that happens is that some potential customers who prefer to rely on common law just don't buy. Every company should see if they cannot de-formalize, and liberalize, contract conditions.

The auditor is recommended to cross-check the information derived to complete this list with the questions and answers in the final List 24, 'Product/service financial information', where the call for data, usually in a slightly different form, occurs.

4.1 Grade the following. Indicate major items in each list. (See Introduction to List 1, 'Marketing strategy and planning', and Question 1.21.)

	STRENGTHS ... WEAKNESSES					
	Major strength	Significant strength	Average	Needs improving	Poor	Major weakness
Manufacturing efficiency						
Quality and consistency						
Technical expertise (R & D problem-solving, etc.)						
Price competitiveness						
Service						
Delivery						
Marketing (and selling) skills						
Size and/or location of operation						
Reputation						
Track record						
Financial position						
Visibility						
Links with customers or suppliers						
Other significant factors (name)						

4.2 Does our sales message and non-personal promotion emphasize our strengths and minimize our weaknesses? (Compare with List 11, 'Non-personal promotion: methods and media', Question 11.33.)

4.3 Indicate annual sales by units and/or value of the products/services under review for the past three to five years.

4.4 What percentage of our output by units or value were to:

Government _____

Direct to end-users (broken down by industry and/or application) _____

Sold to original equipment manufacturers (OEMs) _____

Sold through intermediaries other than OEMs (e.g., merchants, distributors) _____

Exports _____

In-feeding (consumption or utilization of own product/service) _____

TOTAL

_____

(This answer and the next one should be used for comparison purposes with List 7, 'Market size and structure', Question 7.1, and will in any event be needed to complete List 16, 'User industries', Question 16.34.)

4.5 National and regional breakdown of sales if relevant. (See Introduction and Appendix 4A and the answer to List 9, 'The sales force', Questions 9.34 and 9.38.)

4.6 Do sales targets exist for each salesman's/agents/distributors territory? (A detailed answer to this and Questions 4.7 and 4.8 will be required in List 9, 'The sales force', for Questions 9.34–9.38.)

4.7 How were they arrived at? Are they still valid? (See List 9, 'The sales force', Question 9.35, which is the same point.)

4.8 Sales broken down by each sales territory against target (List 7, 'Market size and structure', Question 7.13, and List 9, 'The sales force', Question 9.38, will require these same data):

| | Year (or period) | |
Territory	Target	Achievement

4.9 Sales broken down by product/service characteristics (e.g., sizes, weights, dimensions, specifications) or any other meaningful breakdown including equipment, spares, and service charges. (The answer may have already been given in List 2, 'Product/service range', Question 2.2, and will be asked again in List 7, 'Market size and structure', Question 7.10 and List 9, 'The sales force', Question 9.55. They should all align, of course.)

4.10 Sales broken down by user industry/application. (See Introduction to List 7, 'Market size and structure', Questions 7.10 and 7.11, the former asking the same question.)

4.11 Sales breakdown in percentage terms:

To new users/customers

For new usage among existing customers

As replacement sales

TOTAL	100%

(The answer to this question will be needed for a number of other purposes in due course: List 9, 'The sales force', Question 9.76; List 15, 'Introducing new products/services', Question 15.5; List 16, 'User industries', Questions 16.6 and 16.8; List 22, 'Non-differentiated products', Question 22.17.)

4.12 What is the maximum and average order size for the products/services under review?

4.13 How does profitability vary by order size?

4.14 Based on this, can we produce a model showing the impact on profit of different products/services and order size mix to establish an optimum mix as a marketing/market target? (See List 2, Product/service range', Question 2.5.)

4.15 What is the extent of our own uptake and/or reciprocal trading? State period covered. (This answer will also be required for List 7, 'Market size and structure', Question 7.29, and see the Introduction to that list.)

4.16 Percentage of sales on products introduced in last:

- One year
- Two years
- Three years
- More than three years

(Compare answer with those to List 2, 'Product/service range', Question 2.4, and List 15, 'Introducing new products/services', Questions 15.1 and 15.25.)

4.17 Is the rate of successful introductions comparable to the industry standard? Does it suggest that a change is needed?

4.18 What is the explanation for the performance figures shown?

4.19 What market weaknesses does it indicate (e.g., too heavily weighted in any particular area, or sector, or customer; new/repeat business ratio; inadequate geographic or industry coverage; lack of counter-cyclical business, etc.)?

4.20 What is the proportion of new customers to repeat business (e.g., numbers, volume, value)? (See List 9, 'The sales force', Questions 9.75 and 9.76, relative to this and the previous question and also the answer to Question 4.10 in this list.)

4.21 What are the safe limits (e.g., 40–60%)?

4.22 Does the analysis indicate that a change is required in product/service range composition, selling or promotional methods and/or message, segmentation priorities, customer types, distribution methods, etc.?

4.23 What is, or should be, the normal lead time (period from receipt of order to customer's receipt of goods) and/or start-up offered? (See also List 12, 'The distributive system', Questions 12.41 and 12.45 and List 16, 'User industries', Introduction.)

4.24 What is our conversion ratio of enquiries to quotations? (See also List 11, 'Non-personal promotion: methods and media', Introduction.)

4.25 What is our conversion ratio of enquiries to orders? (These last two very important questions are asked again in List 9, 'The sales force', Questions 9.47 and 9.48, but the data are extended by the addition in that section of Question 9.46.)

4.26 What does the average quotation cost us to prepare?

4.27 What proportion of our business is transacted through distributors? (A more detailed answer will be sought in List 12, 'The distributive system', Questions 12.3 and 12.27.)

4.28 Has this varied over the last three to five years?

4.29 What is the explanation for this variation?

4.30 Does the explanation call for changes in marketing, markets, or products?

4.31 How does profitability on distributor sales compare with profitability on direct sales?

4.32 How do sales costs to distributors compare with sales costs for direct customers?

4.33 What would be the effect in both profit and marketing terms of increasing/decreasing distributor support? (The previous seven questions should be used in conjunction with List 12, 'The distributive system'.)

4.34 How 'visible' is the company and/or its brands? (See Introduction. This answer is also required in List 21, 'Images and perceptions', Question 21.14.)

4.35 What system exists for tracing sources of enquiries?

4.36 Are all members of the firm who receive enquiries required to probe and report on information sources used by potential clients?

4.37 Of these data exist how are they circulated and used?

4.38 Why do our customers buy from us? What are our differentiating advantages? (See Introduction and general comments on differentiation in List 22, 'Non-differentiated products'.)

4.39 Are our terms of business too demanding, restrictive, or antipathetic? (See also List 5, 'Export marketing', Question 5.58.)

4.40 Which of our terms of business would we be prepared to litigate on?

4.41 What would be the risks and benefits of de-formalizing business terms? (See Introduction relative to these last three questions.)

4.42 Do we have a policy on 'own brand' supply?

4.43 How do we justify it? (See also List 12, 'The distributive system', Question 12.72.)

Appendix 4A.   Market share by territory, user industry or applications

Area territory User industry or applications	Market size units and/or value	Market share	Total competitive volume and/or value	Existing no. of accounts	No. of potential accounts

List 5. Export marketing

Introduction

Check lists have an unfortunate proclivity to spawn sub-check lists—something that this book attempts to avoid. However, in the case of exporting so much is involved that the rule has to be bent, most particularly in regard to Question 5.19. Throughout industry, export markets tend to be of the Topsy school ('just grow'd'), the result of an approach from the market or else a selection on the most arbitrary basis; senior management like the country or speak the language, or have relations and friends there. This is not an exaggeration. In making a decision on territories there are more than 100 separate factors to consider, and perhaps as many countries to choose from.

Because markets are as much a part of the firm's resources as its machinery, materials, men, and money, their selection and nurturing is part of marketing resource realization. For this reason, although not central to the internal marketing audit but very much part of the whole marketing activity, this list includes what is both a marketing and a marketing audit check questionnaire.

There are many aids for exporting, some of them heavily subsidized by government, and it will be a very foolish marketing department that did not make it its business to be fully appraised of what is available. Question 5.6 refers only to the British Overseas Trade Board,[1] but there are many others; for example, the Irish Export Board and Industrial Development Authority. However, in pursuit of free or cheap assistance valuable commercial services should not be ignored. Service 800 and the American WATS (Wide Area Telephone Service) enable a customer or prospect to make a direct telephone enquiry over any distance, nationally and internationally, for the cost of a local call.

The choice of markets depends on a knowledge of very many factors, as Question 5.19 implies. The complexity of the task of choosing which territory to attack and the way that it is serviced is so daunting that most firms totally ignore the problem and operate on a reactive or historical basis. What is required is a methodology for acquiring, analysing, and interpreting a mass of material concerning a large number of territories. One such approach has been included as an appendix to this list. The inclusion of the 100+ questions within the main list would be more confusing than helpful. Nevertheless their relegation to an appendix is not intended as a comment on their importance.

There is no reason not to apply many of the questions formulated in the other lists, but it is of particular importance, because of the complications of communication, to ensure that, whatever form of representation is chosen, the representative is aware of what is expected of

1. The leaflet *BOTB Services*, published by the British Overseas Trade Board, details all services available to exporters such as their subsidized market research, subsidized market entry, and marketing advisory services.

him or his company and that the supplier is equally aware of what he in turn is supposed to do. Question 5.28 and Stage 6 of Appendix 5A cover this. The cost of appointing distributors and servicing them is high and a loss of distributor serious. Most losses that are not caused by bad appointments in the first place are the result of neglect, not under-performance. Appointing distributors and agents should receive the same care as appointing any senior staff, and induction is equally important.

In relation to Question 5.31, few exporters realize that the BBC will publicize without charge new product offers to a world-wide audience of 75 million people in 120 countries who listen regularly to the overseas service.

In many overseas territories the choice of agent/distributor is very narrow and may in fact be the decision of the distributor rather than the supplier. The loss of a distributor under these circumstances can equate with the loss of the market. Increasingly, good distributors are being tied in with good suppliers, leaving the less successful as the only choice. This is a situation that can be avoided.

Non-tariff barriers are among the most difficult constraints to identify and circumvent, since they are often unofficial and often impossible to avoid. Japan, for example, has succeeded in introducing a wide range of these defensive measures while denying both their existence and that they are in fact barriers. To some exporters the American product liability requirements are also seen as non-tariff barriers. The existence of such blockages needs careful appraisal because they can easily eliminate what on the face of it seems to be an excellent market opportunity. Behind Question 5.46 may lie the decision of whether to attempt to penetrate any particular market.[2]

The check list steps on to forbidden ground with Question 5.47, which deals with bribery. It is useless to pretend that this is not a method of doing business in many overseas territories, and it would be hypocritical to suggest that it is unknown in the home market. The check list is amoral and takes no attitude on what a firm does when approached for an inducement or in volunteering such inducements. Each firm must decide for itself and, more importantly, must be sure that those who represent it understand and comply with the policy. If the kitchen is too hot . . .

Finally, the check list touches on a frequently overlooked opportunity for companies, especially in geographical areas where market penetration is difficult or impossible. This is licensing. For many companies licensing could increase overseas earnings at minimum risk and investment. That is not to suggest that licensing is necessarily a simple or indeed cheap method of operation. Questions 5.50–5.58 pose some key issues in considering what and how to license. Every company should look to their skills and resources to ensure that they are not in fact missing what could be a useful way of generating new revenues.

---

2. Some guidance can be obtained from the Overseas Tariffs and Regulations (OTAR) section of the Export Data Branch of the British Overseas Trade Board (London).

5.1 Are our products/services capable of meeting an overseas demand?

5.2 On what information is the answer based? Is it recent?

5.3 What changes would be needed in (i) product or range, (ii) overseas facilities, (iii) overseas representations to meet an overseas demand? (See List 24, 'Product/service financial information', Question 24.28.)

5.4 If our products/services are exportable, what reasons exist for not seeking export markets?

5.5 Are the reasons valid under present conditions?

5.6 Do we have full knowledge of the various government schemes and organizations giving financial aid and/or advice and information to assist market research or market entry? (See Introduction and reference to British Overseas Trade Board's publication, *BOTB Services*, and List 6, 'Marketing information: systems and use', Question 6.27.)

5.7 Do we have information on commercial and trade association services to aid export performances? (See also answer to List 6, 'Marketing information: systems and use', Questions 6.21 and 6.27 relative to market information and List 19, 'Industry contacts', Questions 19.3 and 19.6.)

5.8 Where have our exports been obtained? Specify regions and turnover.

		Value/units	
	Year 1	Year 2	This year

e.g., EEC

Rest of Western Europe

Eastern Europe

North America

Central and South America

Africa

Middle East

Australiasia

South-East Asia

Far East

Others (specify)

5.9 Which are presently the top three export countries? Indicate product(s) and markets served.

5.10 How can we account for this performance?

5.11 On what basis were the territories originally selected? (Compare with answer to Question 5.23.)

5.12 Was the basis for selection sound, and is it still valid?

5.13 Did we develop the market or were we approached?

5.14 What marketing actions did we take?

5.15 How successful were they?

5.16 In which of the countries to which we are currently exporting is turnover expected to increase significantly over the next two to three years? (This answer should align with that to List 8, 'Future market', Question 8.24.)

5.17 How far will such an increase be the result of our efforts?

5.18 Could our efforts significantly change the position?

5.19 Indicate additional countries for which export markets are (or will be) sought.

5.20 Why these countries? (See Appendix 5A.)

5.21 How are present export markets served?

	Proportion of total export sales (%)
Forming or acquiring own company in territory	
Direct representation (full-time representative in domicile)	
Regular visits by UK based staff	
Distributor (acting as principal and carrying stocks)	
Agent selling on our behalf	
Franchise agreement outlets	
Joint venture	
License	
Federation[1]	

5.22 Which form of representation is preferred and why?

5.23 What factors were considered in the selection of representative, and was each significant factor correctly weighted? (See Introduction, Question 5.11, and Appendix 5A.)

5.24 Are territory performances evaluated regularly, and by what criteria? (See Appendix 5A, Stage 8.)

5.25 What happens in an under-performance situation?

5.26 Are there formal agreements and contracts with agents/distributors?

5.27 If not, would it be advantageous to formalize arrangements?

5.28 Have we listed the major performance and commercial clauses for any agreement, and do they contain safeguards for us and the agent/distributor?

5.29 What direct knowledge (i.e., not through the distributor/agent) do we have of the market?

5.30 What is the source of that knowledge?

1. Federated marketing is the setting up of an overseas facility by a group of suppliers in the exporting country who sell broadly to the same customers. The costs and risks of market entry are shared and partly underwritten.

5.31 How are enquiries/orders generated in the territories concerned (e.g., personal selling, advertising, public relations, sales visits, etc., not known)? (See Introduction.)

5.32 When were the territories last visited?

5.33 By whom?

5.34 Is the managerial rank of the visitor commensurate with the market potential of the territory?

5.35 When are the next visits planned?

5.36 Has the agent/distributor been invited to visit us?

5.37 If not, why not?

5.38 If so, has he accepted? If not, why not?

5.39 How much of our business is indirect exports?

5.40 What form does it take (main customers and types)?

5.41 Can this type of business be stimulated by marketing in the ultimate country of destination?

5.42 How important are consultants and/or buying agents for direct and indirect exports? (See Introduction to List 2, 'Product/service range', and answers to Questions 2.19–2.22, and List 7, 'Market size and structure', Question 7.32.)

5.43 Does our marketing to consultants/buying agents reflect their importance? (See Introduction to List 2, 'Product/service range', on 'indirect marketing'.)

5.44 How important are government and para-statal bodies in decision-making?

5.45 Are our contacts with government at the right level?

5.46 What non-tariff barriers exist? (See Introduction.)

5.47 How endemic are bribery and other inducements in influencing business?

5.48 What is our policy on this?

5.49 Are all members of the firm informed of this policy?

(The answers to questions 5.50–5.58 should be cross-checked with those in List 15, 'Introducing new products/services', Questions 15.43–15.58.)

5.50 Is it possible to license any of our products, our production methods, application know-how, patents, trade names, or designs?

5.51 Can we export the high-technology components of our product(s) and license less critical assemblies?

5.52 Are there opportunities for cross-licensing that would provide new products for home or export markets? (See answer to List 15, 'Introducing new products/services', Question 15.42.)

5.53 What factors must exist to make a licence arrangement profitable (e.g., high transport costs, trade barriers, lack of marketing and financial resource, lack of territorial knowledge, inability to provide back-up services, market preference for indigenous or favoured nation suppliers)?

5.54 What conditions will we attach to our licence (e.g., minimum sales or royalty payments, down payment, territorial limitations, access to production methods, access to accounts, no marketing of competitive licensed or merchanted products)?

5.55 How big must the local market be to justify granting a licence? (See List 7, 'Market size and structure'.)

5.56 How will we police licence agreements?

5.57 Can we prevent licensor from re-selling license to third countries without our knowledge or agreement?

5.58 Can we develop a form of licence agreement that is comprehensive, practical and legally acceptable in the countries of the licensors but is not so restrictive as to deter would-be licensees? (See Introduction and List 4, 'Company performance', Questions 4.39–4.41.)

Appendix 5A. A method for the selection of export territories and export representation[1]

Introduction

Marketing—industrial or consumer—does not differ in its basic approach in any country of the world, but the variations involved in meeting the unique conditions of each market are as numerous as the markets themselves. Different messages, different tools, different media—indeed, different human beings—may well be critical for achieving success. The danger of assuming that a successful marketing system or approach in the home market will be equally successful in a foreign market is too obvious to need stating, and yet, this is precisely what most companies attempting export markets in fact assume.

Success in export markets depends heavily on a company's willingness to adjust to the market's needs in terms of products and the market's receptivity in terms of communication methods and message. Culture clash, differences in levels of sophistication and business literacy, and confusion of the relationship of marketing response to marketing effort can lead to under-achievement on a massive scale.

Thus, in the study of export markets it is necessary to have a real understanding of the markets that, in the final analysis, even with industrial products, comprise people rather than things. Moreover, since all companies have limited resources for marketing, it is even more vital to select only that number of markets which can be successfully penetrated with the appropriations available.

Any decision to export involving the choice of a territory and the appointment of a foreign representative or agent pre-empts an important preceding step, which is to have a long hard look at what the company has to offer the market (see Questions 5.1–5.5). Is the product suitable; will the price be competitive; can the company provide the back-up service and sales support that will be needed; what, if any, minimum stock levels will be required; what payments terms are reasonable and how do they compare with the competition; are resources available to allow a territory selected to be visited regularly? Answers to all these questions were called for in the list. Of equal importance is how much the appointed representative can reasonably be expected to earn, and whether it would be commensurate with the time investment (and possibly money) allowing for the build-up and consolidation period. The representative will certainly ask, either as an individual or corporately, 'what's in it for me?' and the company must have the answer and be sure that an alternative use of the representative's time and money would not be more profitable for him. The representative with a long list of principals of which only the profitable few receive his attention is an all too common feature of the export scene.

Thus a decision on representation must be preceded by an evaluation of the

---

1. The terms 'representative' and 'agent' are used interchangeably, but it should be noted that in some territories they have distinctive meanings. 'Representative' can imply a full-time direct employee of the exporting company, and 'agent', a freelance person or organization usually rewarded on a commission basis.

company's products, the agency agreement, the terms of trade, etc., aimed at making the representation attractive and profitable both for the principal and for the representative.

Stage 1   To export or not to export

It may be that a company does not believe that it has an exportable product. Clearly, in those circumstances the decision is obvious, but the facts leading to that conclusion should nevertheless be marshalled and double-checked.

In contra distinction, some markets offer such obvious and substantial possibilities that there is little point in undertaking the screening exercise that follows. Developments within a territory—the discovery of a basic raw material, the construction of a new type of plant such as water distillation, or the injection of foreign aid funds for specific projects—may produce what is called an 'availability effect', that is, to make the creation of other industries feasible and viable. This in turn may open up substantial if obvious opportunities. In these circumstances the territorial decision is again pre-empted.

Stage 2   Which territory?

Having made a decision to export, given that neither of the two pre-emptions referred to above apply, then the question to be decided is which territory or territories represent the best potential market. Questions 5.11, 5.16, 5.19, and 5.20 refer to this point.

The decision is not an easy one and most certainly will differ for each company. An export screen is shown on pages 45–46 which aims to provide management with some guidelines as to the attractiveness of territories compared with each other; this screen can be re-used when reviewing the factors affecting the achieved performance in a particular territory.

Screen 1 is concerned with non-controllable external factors which might eliminate a country that otherwise could appear to be satisfactory on the many points in Screen 2. Thus, Screen 1 is intended to remove countries that would not warrant deeper investigation before that investigation takes place.

Screen 3 is also an eliminating grid but, unlike Screen 1, is intended to be specific to the company making the analysis. The suggested items for consideration are no more than examples of the sort of issues that ought to be considered. Each company must develop its own factors for Screen 3. It should be borne in mind however, that, unlike Screen 1, the company may well have some control over the items involved if it so chooses.

The point about Screens 1 and 3 is that, no matter how heavily they are weighted and rated on the system described below, they could still not be sufficiently depressed to eliminate a territory automatically. These two screens, 1 and 3, are used to ensure that any extra heavy impact of the aspects listed are not accidentally diffused in the main screen. Where Screen 2 indicates an otherwise favourable territory situation, the company may wish to consider adjustments to the factors in Screen 3 that might otherwise eliminate a market.

As for Screen 2, a good deal of the information required can be obtained from three source books.[2] Note that all the open-ended questions seek an answer as to whether the subject of the question is favourable for the exporting company in that destination country. Thus, in answering factor 2, which refers to the development plan of a country, the question means 'does it favour the company's product?' As an example, if the

---

2. *World Markets Workbook*, Binder Hamlyn Fry & Co. Ltd, London; *World Index of Economic Forecasts*, Gower Press, Farnborough, Hampshire; *International Directory of Published Market Research*, Arlington Management Publications, London.

territory were Singapore, with a large off-shore oil search programme, it would likely be a plan that would encourage a turbine or open steel flooring manufacturing company. An opposite situation might occur. As labour is desperately short, any indication in the forward plan of immigration restrictions would indicate an unfavourable position to any labour-intensive activity.

Many questions can be safely deleted. For example, a manufacturer of an industrial product could ignore factors 17 and 18. If the decision as to the form of representation does not involve setting up a local company with premises, then factors like 49—'Cost of land'—can be deleted as well as factors 50–62.

Hence this screen is not quite so formidable when the inapplicable factors are deleted.

Weighting and rating

The next step is to decide on the weight of any one factor in relation to others, and it is recommended to use a simple 1–2–3 basis: 3 is important and 1 is unimportant. Any finer scale will only tend to confuse the issue. Thus, for example, the gross national product and growth rate (factor 1) would be rated 3 by most companies, as would question 10, 'Size of market'. 'Price levels', factor 15, perhaps would be 2, and factor 6, 'Balance of payments outlook', 1.

Taking the first four factors as an example, the weightings might appear as follows:

3 for 'GNP growth'
2 for 'Nature of development plan'
3 for 'resistance to recession'
1 for 'relative dependence on imports/exports'

After the weighting comes the rating, which aims to decide how the individual country rates on the point under consideration. Here it is important to use a negative and positive scale, usually $+2$ to -2. If 'positive only' scales are used, a heavily *weighted* factor multiplies up a low *rated* factor to a better position. For example, take weighting 3 on a very poor rating 1: using only a positive scale (where 'bad' is rated 1) gives $3 \times 1 = 3$, while on the $+$ and $-$ scale a heavy weighting on a bad rating gives $3 \times -2 = -6$, providing an appropriately low position. Thus the scales might be:

$+2$ excellent
$+1$ good
0 average or fair
-1 poor
-2 bad

For Screens 1 and 3 much heavier weightings will be needed for factors which on their own do not indicate the elimination of a country (e.g., political barriers). Here, numerical weightings of perhaps as high or higher than $+10$ to -10 may be needed.

Thus the ratings on the first four questions might look like this:

Question	Territory rating					
	A	B	C	D	E	F
1	+2	0	+1	−2	+1	+1
2	0	−1	−2	0	+1	−1
3	+2	+1	−2	0	−2	+2
4	+1	+1	0	+2	−1	+2

Now if the weights are applied, they total like this:

Question	Weighting	Territory weighted ratings					
		A	B	C	D	E	F
1	3	+6	0	+3	−6	+3	+3
2	2	0	−2	−4	0	+2	−2
3	3	+6	+3	−6	0	−6	+6
4	1	+1	+1	0	+2	−1	+2
		+13	+2	−7	−4	−2	+9

From this analysis, on the first four questions territory 'A' looks best. The system continues to the end and the final totals are compared. It is emphasized that a difference of two or three points in the total is not significant. What the screen aims to do is to separate the excellent from the average or poor—not much more.

Screen 1 having been applied before using Screen 2, the first eliminations will have taken place. If the top scoring territories in Screen 2 are now final-checked against Screen 3, the best territories for further consideration or action will be clearly seen.

Stage 3 Form of representation

The next step after the selection of the territory is to decide what form of representation to use. To some extent, the choice of territory will also govern the form of representation. For example, no agents are currently permitted to operate in Algeria; Indonesia demands full local participation; suitable local representatives may just not exist in some Gulf states. Question 5.21 gave the major alternatives for consideration, which are:

- Own company in territory
- Home-based representatives travelling to the territory
- Directly employed representatives residing in the territory
- Local agents
- Distributor representation
- Forming, acquiring, licensing, or franchising a foreign individual or organization
- Joint venture
- Federation

Stage 4 Profiling the optimum representative (or organization)

Criteria will be necessary to assist in the decision as to what type of representation will be adopted. For example, if there is a need to hold minimum stock levels in the territory this will almost certainly eliminate an agency arrangement in favour of a distributor; the requirement for frequent end-customer contact at technical level will imply the use of directly employed local resident representatives. Quite obviously, the development of these criteria needs careful thought to ensure that all facets of the exporting trading activity are listed and considered.

Stage 5 Screening the candidates

The next step is to devise a screen from which all representation candidates/organizations are passed in order to aid the selection of the best one. Again, the factors to be considered require development within the exporting company, and the need for product training and level of marketing/sales support should not be overlooked.

As with the country selection, a system of weighting and rating is recommended so that each candidate is considered on a quantified merit basis and comparisons are thus reasonably accurate. (Tangentially, designing a screen of this type assists considerably in conducting a structured and disciplined interview with each candidate or asking them the correct questions in correspondence.)

The use of any screen, of course, ignores the question of whether the representation will be attractive enough to tempt the candidate who comes out top of the rating. In looking at the problem substantially from the exporting company's point of view, the attraction of their offer to the potential representative is not a factor to be ignored.

Stage 6 Performance standards

It is desirable to develop quantified performance standards and operational procedures with representatives at the time of their initial appointment, or at the very least to agree that standards of performance will be devised as the relationship develops, and that achievement of these standards and conformance with procedures will be critical in the annual review on which continuation or severance of the arrangement will be based. Questions 5.26–5.28 cover this. In setting standards, the candidate must agree that they are reasonable and the exporting company will need to be certain that the minimum standard they set will justify their investment in time and money in servicing the representation.

Stage 7 Locating candidates: Sources of information

Clearly, the greater the number of potential representatives for consideration, the greater the chance of locating one close to the criteria established. Thus, multiple sources of information need to be approached. A number of suggested sources including advertising follow, but each company should seek to add to the list:

- Chamber of Commerce—home, foreign–joint, local in the selected territory
- Exhibitions
- Visiting trade missions
- Customers
- Advertising in local and foreign journals read in the territory
- Marketing and management associations in the territory
- Other agents[3]
- Commercial departments of embassies and high commissions
- Trade associations—home and in the territory
- Foreign embassies
- Banks and financial institutions
- Associations of agents or distributors

In addition, the use of press releases in the territory could stimulate enquiries for handling the representation; e.g., the announcement of a new product or product availability and a statement that the company is seeking representatives in the territory has been found to stimulate responses.

---

3. This group subdivides:
   (i) Agents approached but who are not appointed, because of either their lack of interest or their unsuitability
   (ii) Other existing agents (particularly within organizations that have different operating companies) covering the same territories

Stage 8 Monitoring performance

The final step is the development of an evaluation procedure to enable performance to be monitored and to ensure that the minimum performance standards are in keeping with any change in the exporting company, with new opportunities in the territory, and with other influencing factors that will legitimately increase or decrease the targeted performance (Question 5.24).

It is vital that every effort should be made to avoid losses of representatives since the cost of appointment and lost opportunities is considerable. Reasons for less than satisfactory performance should be analysed, and only if the position is unlikely to be improved should termination by either side be considered. Any breakdown in relationships must be detected in time to enable the reasons for disenchantment to be analysed and corrective action taken where possible.

There is a world shortage of competent representatives, and those that a company has appointed should be nurtured and motivated so that their activities will be mutually profitable.

The discipline of a formal and regular agency/distributor review meeting which looks beyond immediate activities or enquiries, quotations, and contracts and considers the performance and relationship in depth is most likely to produce ideas that will improve the total export performance of a company.

Conclusion

The level of company resource will, of course, dictate the degree of sophistication that can be employed in the development of an export strategy and exporting objectives. It appears to be well proven that the highest rewards follow a policy of concentration and the avoidance of any attempt to spread the total marketing management and its resources too thinly over too many territories.

Screening potential export territories

Screen 1 Eliminating factors

Unacceptable product	(Standards, safety, socio-cultural factors)
Political barriers	(Boycotts, sanctions, local participation, state monopolies)
Economic	(Non-transferability of funds, barter trading, price levels)
Legal	(Anti trust legislation, labour laws, patents, environmental control)
Supply	(Shortage of labour/materials, distributors/servicing)

Screen 2 General influencing factors

			Individual countries								
			A		B		C		D		
Group	Factor	Weighting	Rating	Total	Rating	Total	Rating	Total	Rating	Total	
Economic	1. Size of GNP and rate of growth 2. Nature of development plan 3. Resistance to recession 4. Relative dependence on imports and exports 5. Foreign exchange position 6. Balance of payments outlook 7. Stability of currency, convertibility 8. Remittance and repatriation regulations 9. Balance of economy (industry–agriculture–trade) 10. Size of market for products; rate of growth 11. Size of population; rate of growth 12. *Per capita* income; rate of growth 13. Income distribution 14. Current or prospective membership in a customs union 15. Price levels; rate of inflation										
Political	16. Stability of government; its form 17. Presence or absence of class antagonism 18. Special political, ethnic, and social problems 19. Attitude towards private and foreign investment 20. Acceptability of foreign investment by government 21. Acceptability of foreign investment by customers and competitors 22. Presence or absence of nationalization threat 23. Presence or absence of state industries 24. Do state industries receive favoured treatment? 25. Concentration of influence in small groups 26. 'Most favoured nation' treatment availability										
Government	27. Fiscal and monetary policies 28. Extent of bureaucratic interference and administration 29. Fairness and honesty of administrative procedures 30. Degree of anti-foreign discrimination 31. Fairness of courts 32. Clear and modern corporate investment laws 33. Patentability of product 34. Presence or absence of price controls 35. Restriction on complete or majority ownership										
Geographic	36. Efficiency of transport system and methods 37. Port facilities[1] 38. Free ports, free zones, bonded warehouses[1] 39. Proximity to export markets 40. Proximity to suppliers, customers 41. Proximity to raw material sources 42. Existing supporting industry 43. Availability of local raw material 44. Availability of power, water, gas 45. Reliability of utilities 46. Waste disposal facilities 47. Ease of exporting 48. Ease of importing 49. Cost of suitable land										

1. And level of costs.

Group	Factor	Weighting	Individual countries							
			A		B		C		D	
			Rating	Total	Rating	Total	Rating	Total	Rating	Total
Labour	50. Availability of managerial, technical, official personnel 51. Availability of skilled labour 52. Availability of semi skilled and unskilled labour 53. Level of worker productivity 54. Training facilities 55. Outlook for increase in labour supply 56. Degree of skill and discipline at all levels 57. Climate of labour relations 58. Degree of labour involvement in management 59. Compulsory and voluntary fringe benefits 60. Social security taxes 61. Total cost of labour, including fringe benefits 62. Compulsory or customary profit-sharing									
Tax	63. Tax rates (corporate and personal income, capital, withholding, turnover, VAT, excise, payroll, capital gains, customs, other indirect, and local taxes) 64. General tax morality 65. Fairness and incorruptibility of tax authorities 66. Long-term trend for taxes 67. Taxation of export income earned abroad 68. Tax incentives for new business 69. Depreciation rates 70. Tax loss carry forward and back 71. Joint tax treaties 72. Duty and tax drawbacks 73. Availability of tariff protection									
Capital	74. Availability of local capital 75. Costs of local borrowing 76. Normal terms for local borrowing 77. Availability of convertible currencies locally 78. Efficiency of banking system 79. Government credit aids to new business 80. Availability and cost of export financing including insurance 81. Do normal loan sources (US, European, Japanese, international agencies) favour investment?									
Business methods	82. General business morality 83. State of development of marketing and distribution system 84. Normal profit margins, for industry concerned 85. Climate of competition 86. Antitrust and restrictive practices laws 87. Quality of life for expatriate staff									

Screen 3 Specific influencing factors (for the individual company)

Group	Factor	Weighting	Individual countries							
			A		B		C		D	
			Rating	Total	Rating	Total	Rating	Total	Rating	Total
	Company and trade mark must be well known. A good geographical network of distributor/service companies must exist. No conflict must occur with corporate development elsewhere in company's markets. Reasonable level of local management sophistication. Must not compete with company's customers also exporting/producing in the area. Internal transportation capable of handling products.									
	Score:									

List 6. Marketing information: systems and use

Introduction

This list, perhaps like the ones concerned with company performance, sales, and other financial analyses, is the most difficult to contain in length since information is the key to profitable action and there is an insatiable demand for more information. That is not to say that the information gathered is always used or, if used, used well. On the contrary: it has long been recognized that an appeal for more information is about the best excuse to postpone a decision, and market research the best reason ever devised for not making a decision at all.

The whole self-conducted market audit fails if there is not the information to answer the questions posed, so in a sense this section is a key to the success of the technique. Indeed, many auditors may well want to make this section the first. That it is not was deliberate, however. The interface between perceiving the need for information and the gathering, disseminating, and action process is best appreciated if 'need' is demonstrated, as has been attempted in the previous five sections, before methodology.

Information can be divided into two groups: desk or secondary research, and original field research. In the former group is the information already inside the company, although not perhaps in an immediately usable form. The latter group represents that which must be obtained by external enquiry, usually marketing research. Too many companies rush into the field work without adequate examination of what can be obtained quickly and cheaply internally and which frequently gives data with a far higher degree of accuracy than can be derived from other sources.

One of the most neglected sources of internal information are salesmen's reports. Individually, in aggregate, and over time, they can yield extremely valuable evidence on market conditions and trends. To tap into this rich potential, it is necessary in the first instance to ensure that the report format provides a disciplined approach notably lacking in narrative-type reports, and that it does not encourage such blanket responses for failure as 'price'. Time devoted to developing an easily completed but fully informative reporting form and in encouraging salesmen to complete them is always well invested.

None of this is to imply that the salesmen should be used for market research. This is quite wrong. They are trained to persuade, not to report objectively, but they can and should be motivated to be forward listening posts for the company. By demonstrating the value of the information, both to the firm and to their own activities, it is not difficult to persuade salesmen to provide data not easily obtainable elsewhere and certainly not at such low cost.

From internal records it is usually possible to carry out a number of practical analyses. Ratio, correlation and actuarial analyses required in List 4, 'Company performance', permit reliable appraisals to be made of, for example, competitors' position and markets. There are many excellent books on desk research, and particularly internal research, and on the technique for developing and using different types of analyses. These should be consulted if the auditor feels at a loss to undertake the study required to answer questions that call for sales analyses.

External secondary market information exists in embarrassingly large quantities, and, fortunately, there are a number of good source reference works that can lead the inquirer to the relevant publications. The three books referred to in List 5, 'Export marketing', Appendix 5A, make an excellent start. Additionally, for a company seriously attempting to build up a low-cost but effective information department, organizations such as Aslib (formerly Association of Special Libraries and Information Bureaux) and publications such as *Current Technology Index* and *British National Bibliography* are invaluable.

In order to put some methodology into the search, a Standard Operating Procedure might make a useful starting point.[1]

So far as external market research is concerned, this check list is confined to questions relating to doing or commissioning research and evaluating the results, and not to the questions that the researchers must ask. However, in order to assist the marketing auditor three subsidiary check lists have been added to this section relative to external marketing research. The first is a wide-ranging list of questions to act as an *aide-memoire* in devising instructions and giving objectives to the researchers. It is not suggested that more than the smallest proportion of these questions should be asked, and the auditor or research sponsor needs to select only the vital questions. This list is also available as a separate pamphlet from the British Overseas Trade Board.

The second subsidiary list is a guide covering factors for consideration in choosing an outside agency to undertake the research. In many countries there is a bewildering choice of organizations with widely varying specializations and approaches. This second list suggests some of the operational and resource aspects that ought to be taken into account when making a choice of agency.

The third list relates to Question 6.13, and is a type of litmus test for deciding if the research has achieved its purpose.

The Assessment of Industrial Markets referred to earlier contains a summary of research techniques and suggestions for important information sources.[2]

Underlying each and every question is the need to ensure that responsibility is designated for deciding what information is needed, that the task of finding and disseminating it is allocated, and above all for ensuring that the data gathered are used quickly and effectively. Without this control, information-gathering is either a waste of time or an under-utilized resource. Questions 6.4, 6.5, and 6.25 identify if the situation is satisfactory.

In relation to Question 6.21, the *International Directory of Published Market Research* (see List 5, 'Export marketing', Appendix 5A footnote for details) will provide considerable help and information, but it is always worthwhile inviting major marketing research agencies to place the firm on their mailing lists to be kept informed of multi-client studies available or being undertaken.

Question 6.27 seeks to identify a frequently overlooked source of market opportunity identification. Most of the international agencies provide, on request, information on projects under consideration at every stage from pre-feasibility to commissioning. All companies should ensure that they receive regular notifications of all agencies', governmental

1. Aubrey Wilson, *The Assessment of Industrial Markets*, Associated Business Programmes, London, 1973, pp. 105–8.
2. Ibid., Chapter 5.

and para-statal bodies' activities that might imply a business opportunity. By way of example, the European Development Fund has some £2 billion available as grants or 'soft loans' for aid projects ranging from new airports to the equipment for new science technology centres. Awarding and spending these monies creates a large number of business opportunities for firms who monitor the market position.

A frequent source of waste is the large number of journals, technical publications, and books a company buys or subscribes to and which never get read. A full listing of who receives what will quickly identify material that ought to be read as well as received and what publications are superfluous to the organization's needs. Answering Question 6.36–6.41 can quickly show how efficient and cost-effective the publications subscription list is.

6.1 Are our financial records in a form that permits important and regular sales analyses? (For requirements see Questions in List 4, 'Company performance', and List 24, 'Product/service financial information'.)

6.2 What adjustments could be reasonably incorporated in record-keeping in order to obtain key performance data in relation to markets and marketing?

6.3 What internal and external market and marketing surveillance systems exist? (See also Questions 6.18, 6.21, and 6.27 and List 9, 'The sales force', Question 9.97.)

6.4 Who in the organization is responsible for collection and dissemination of information?

6.5 Does any system exist to check (a) efficiency of collection; (b) accuracy of dissemination; (c) extent of utilization? (See also answer to Questions 6.15, 6.19, and 6.26.)

6.6 What constraints prevent greater exploitation of available information?

6.7 What constraints prevent gathering of more information?

6.8 Do salesmen's reporting forms encourage collection and dissemination of market information? (See Introduction and List 9, 'The sales force', Questions 9.95–9.99.)

6.9 Do service calls provide information on market and individual customer sales opportunities? (See List 3, 'The service element in marketing', Question 3.40.)

6.10 Is responsibility for analysing reports clearly assigned, and do instructions exist as to the persons who are to receive the information derived?

6.11 What marketing research—internal and external—has been undertaken?

6.12 What were the factors considered in deciding to undertake the research internally or externally:

- Special skill requirements
- Need for anonymity
- Need for objectivity
- Existence of special resources or experience
- Requirement for product/service knowledge
- Requirement for knowledge of company and/or its markets
- Nature of research problem
- Advantage of cross-industry fertilization
- Cost
- Timing

6.13 Was the research judged to be successful and profitable? (See Appendix 6C.)

6.14 If not, what should have been done, or not have been done, to make it successful?

6.15 How were the marketing research data utilized? (See answers to Questions 6.5 and 6.26.)

6.16 How does marketing research expenditure compare with competitors' expenditure?

6.17 Can we justify any differences?

6.18 Is there a commercial library or central source of market and marketing information?

6.19 To what extent is it utilized, and does utilization justify the cost of its maintenance?

6.20 If there is no internal information service would it be cost effective to provide one?

6.21 Do we monitor multi-client studies being made available or encourage agencies to undertake the examination of subjects of interest to us? (See Introduction and List 5, 'Export marketing', Question 5.7.)

6.22 Is there a precise specification of the information to be collected regularly?

6.23 How is market information fed into the system?

6.24 Is it disseminated and used quickly?

6.25 Who in the organization receives the information?

6.26 What knowledge and experience do we have of its utilization? (See also answers to questions 6.5, 6.15, and 6.19.)

6.27 Do we possess a comprehensive list of regular market information and market opportunity reports (e.g., British Overseas Trade Board's Export Intelligence Service/European Development Fund projects)? (See answers in List 5, 'Export marketing', Questions 5.6 and 5.7.)

6.28 Which reports do we subscribe to?

6.29 Have we evaluated their worth to the company by checking what actions and results have occurred through using them?

6.30 What information does our trade association supply? (See List 19, 'Industry contacts', Questions 19.2, 19.3, and 19.4.)

6.31 Can we persuade them to initiate a market information service for our industry or to improve any data they already provide? (See List 19, 'Industry contacts', Question 19.6.)

6.32 Would an inter-firm comparison study assist us in evaluating our performance against an industry norm?

6.33 What trend information do we have, and how well is it disseminated and used? (This answer should be used in conjunction with List 8, 'Future market'.)

6.34 What variance information do we have, and how well is it disseminated and used? (Compare answers with those in List 24, 'Product/service financial information', Questions 24.15 and 24.23.)

6.35 Are there any lead or lag indicators that signal future developments and opportunities? (This question is repeated in List 8, 'Future market', Question 8.1.)

6.36 What journals are taken by the company?

6.37 Who receives them?

6.38 What evidence do we have they are (a) read and (b) used?

6.39 Do they cover all areas and markets of interest to the company?

6.40 Can a formal system of reading and reporting be adopted?

6.41 Does a method exist to monitor action on important information circulated?

Appendix 6A. Marketing research

This list contains questions already included in both previous and later sections and which form an essential part of the internal marketing audit. They are repeated here because they could conceivably form part of a marketing research brief and also because some are re-phrased for comparison on a competitive basis.

Market size

1. What is the size of the total market for the product?
2. How durable is the market?
3. What is domestic consumption (volume or value)?
4. What proportion or amount (volume and/or value) is met from domestic production?
5. What proportion or amount (volume and/or value) is met from imported sources?
6. What are the main export markets from (a) domestic production? (b) re-exported imports?
7. What factors limit the size of the total market?
8. What are the sizes of the various market strata?
   - By geographical regions?
   - By size of user?
   - By industry?
   - By type, quality, design or price of product?
   - By type of distributor?
9. What is the size of the total market for a substitute product?
10. What are the export possibilities?

Market structure

1. Who are the main domestic suppliers to the market?
2. Which countries are the main source of imports?
3. Which importing firms are the most important?
4. What is the export performance of main competitors?
5. Which are their main markets?
6. What are the geographical variations in the domestic market?
7. What are the seasonal/cyclical variations in the domestic market?
8. What factors currently favour the emergence of new competitors?
9. What factors are currently likely to lead to the reduction of competitors?
10. Which are the main user industries?
11. Which are the subsidiary user industries?

12. Is in-feeding significant in the user industries?

13. Do reciprocal trading practices exist?

Market trends

1. How does the market size compare with
   - 10 years ago?
   - 5 years ago?
   - last year?
2. How does product demand differ from
   - 10 years ago?
   - 5 years ago?
   - last year?
3. What trends are revealed indicating a shift in demand over the last
   - 10 years?
   - 5 years?
   - year?
4. In what ways are market changes likely to manifest themselves?
5. What changes occurring in the user industries are likely to induce a change in demand?
6. What changes occurring in the non-user industries are likely to induce a new demand?
7. What changes occurring in the firm's products and processes are likely to induce a change in demand?
8. What changes occurring in the economy are likely to affect demand for the firm's products?
   - Levels of employment
   - Levels of income
   - Level of industrial investment
   - Level of industrial profits
   - Industrial dividends
   - Rates of corporate taxation
   - Wholesale prices
   - Level of industrial production
   - Consumers' expenditure
   - Personal savings
   - Rates of personal taxation
   - Retail prices
   - Population trends
   - Rates of interest
   - Credit restrictions
   - Hire-purchase debt
   - Export trends
   - Import trends
   - Balance of payments
9. What trends are likely to attract new entrants into the industry in the future?
10. What trends are likely to reduce the numbers of competitors in the future?
11. Are changes in materials or production methods likely to reduce the need for the product?

Market share

1. What share of the market does the firm command?
2. What are the main competitors' shares?
3. What is the firm's share of the market when broken down
   - By industries?
   - By size of firms?
   - Geographically?
4. What are the main competitor's shares?
   - By industries?
   - By size of firms?
   - Geographically?
5. What share of the market is held by imported products?
6. What factors support the market share of imported products?
7. What percentage of business is from
   - Old customers?
   - New customers?
8. How concentrated or dispersed are sales?

The firm

1. What is the reputation of the firm within the user industries?
2. What is the reputation of the firm's products within these industries?
3. What is the firm's 'image'?
4. What are the firm's individual 'brand images'?
5. Is the name and reputation of the firm established?
6. Do the firm's suppliers form potential markets for its products?
7. Does the firm absorb any of its own products?
8. What services are provided by the firm?
9. How do these relate to market requirements?
10. What guarantees are offered?
11. How advisable is it to brand own products with private brands?
12. What are the critical factors for success (e.g., distributive network 'approvals', local participation, etc.)?

Marketing methods

1. What marketing tools are currently used and how do they compare with the firm's current choice of tools?
2. How does budget percentage in each of the following media compare with competitors'?
   - Newspapers
   - Journals
   - Outdoor
   - Direct mail
   - Exhibitions

- Education campaigns
- Catalogues and brochures
- Public relations campaigns
- Point of sale
- Films
- Sampling
- Others

3. What reasons can be ascribed for any differences?

4. What other tools should be considered?

5. What criteria will be used for rejection or acceptance?

6. What methods of evaluation of total marketing and of individual tools exist?

7. How often is an evaluation of effectiveness made?

8. What is the history of the firm's marketing expenditure in value, and per unit sold?

9. What is the cost of marketing
   - Annually?
   - Per enquiry?
   - Per order?
   - Per salesman?
   - By media?

10. What is the marketing expenditure, broken down by
    - Method?
    - Media?
    - Season?
    - Geographically?
    - Industry?
    - Application?

11. How does the firm's marketing history and performance compare with competitors'?

12. What is the copy strategy used on the firm's products during the last 5 years?

13. What are the major changes and causes of change in copy strategy that have occurred in the last 5 years?

14. To what type of advertising and media are users and potential users most exposed?

15. In what way does competitive advertising differ from the firm's?
    - Media?
    - Frequency?
    - Space?
    - Copy?
    - Strategy?

16. What is the audience (in numbers) for specific methods?

Personal selling

1. What are the usual personal selling methods adopted for the product?

2. What is the history of the firm's personal selling methods?

3. What is the user industry structure, organization, and geographical division for the sale of the product?

4. How does this compare with the firm's usual structure, organization, and geographical division for the sale of the product?

5. What is the sales history of the product in value and volume?

6. How specialized is selling among competitors?

7. If the product is seasonal, can fluctuations be evened out by balancing sales of varying types of products or by buying inducements?

8. What aids do salesmen need?
   - Advertising support
   - Technical advice
   - Marketing data
   - Catalogues
   - Drawings
   - Samples
   - Educational slides or film demonstrations
   - Offers of credit
   - Offers of HP facilities

9. How effectively are tenders handled?

10. What proportion of enquiries are converted to sales?

11. How does this compare with
    - 5 years ago?
    - last year?

12. What is the image of the firm's salesmen?

13. How are salesmen motivated and how does this compare with competitors?

14. Do salesmen concentrate on benefits or features?

15. Is the call reporting form adequate for providing information on customer needs, reactions, and reasons for lost business, etc.?

16. Could the sales reporting form be adapted to provide market information?

17. Is there a reporting-back system to individual salesmen on best and total sales performance?

18. Are salesmen technically qualified?

19. What proportion of total calls are committed to existing customers?

20. How many calls are for new business?

21. How many initial approaches are required, on average, to begin a meaningful dialogue?

22. What is the average number of calls required to secure one order?

23. How many quotations are submitted, on average, in order to obtain one order?

24. What is the average order value for new business?

25. What is the average order value for repeat business?

26. What proportion of calls are made by appointments?

27. How many telephone canvass calls are made in a day?

28. How many telephone canvass calls are required, on average, to secure one appointment?

29. How many letters are sent to prospects each day?

30. What proportion of these are followed up by phone or by a visit?

31. What proportion of letters produce a response without follow-up?

Distribution methods

1. Approximately how many distributors of the product are there in the market as a whole?
2. How effective are the distributive methods used?
3. How do they compare with competitors' distributive methods?
4. What alternatives exist?
5. What is the division of the firm's sales by
   - Each type of distributor?
   - Size of distributor?
   - Geographical location of distributors?
   - Industrial concentration of distributors?
6. What percentage of total sales for each product is directly transacted with users?
7. What is the history of the introduction of the product and the sequence of marketing steps that led to its present distribution?
8. What is the replenishment lead time?
9. What is the history of 'out-of-stock' situations?
10. What stocks are normally held at the plant?
    - Average
    - Seasonal
11. What stocks are normally in the distributive pipeline?
12. How far do distributors handle service, maintenance, spares, etc.?
13. How far do distributors handle competitors' service, maintenance, spares, etc.?
14. How technically competent are distributors?
15. Are franchise and exclusive dealing arrangements prevalent?
16. Are the distributive outlets the most efficient available?
17. How effective are distributors' selling efforts?
18. What aids do competitors give to distributors?
19. How do the firm's aids to distributors compare with those offered by competitors?
20. To what extent do distributors concentrate on the product group?
21. To what extent are distributors verticalized?
22. What other types of product do they handle?
23. What types of customer/industry do they supply to (e.g. across all industries; only to small customers)?
24. Do distributors influence the *make* of products purchased by the end-user?
25. Is the role of the distributor increasing, decreasing, or remaining constant in importance in the market under review?
26. Do distributors compete for customers with their suppliers? If so, to what degree?
27. What is the size of discounts offered to distributors?
    - By the firm?
    - By competitors?

Shipment and packaging

1. How is the package shipped?
2. How do the firm's physical transport methods compare with competitors'?
   - Cost
   - Speed
   - Liability to damage
   - Liability to pilferage
3. What are the comparative shipping costs and times using alternative methods?
4. Would standard pack dimensions reduce cost of shipment?
5. Is the package destroyed, returned or re-used?
6. Is the package used to hold contents until empty, or is it immediately emptied?
7. Should the package have a dispensing device?
8. What is the average amount of contents used on each occasion?
9. Is other material subsequently stored in the package?
10. At what distance must the package be identified?
11. How is identification of contents achieved?
12. How is the package handled in the stockroom, on the factory floor and elsewhere?
13. How long is a package held in stock?
14. What content protection measures are necessary?
15. What pack protective measures are required against damage in transit and storage by vermin, moisture, temperature, pilferage?
16. How are empties stored?
17. How is the package handled in storage and shipment?
18. What is the history of delayed deliveries?
19. Are customers informed when the product is dispatched and by what route or carrier?
20. How far are late deliveries caused by delayed dispatches and how far by slow transport methods or handling?
21. Are customers made aware of delays caused by carriers?

Profit

1. What is the profit history of the product?
2. What is the unit profit history?
3. What is known about profits of other manufacturers in the same field?
4. What contribution to profits of other products does the product make?
5. What non-profit advantages does the firm derive?
6. What changes in profits have changes in marketing strategy achieved in the last 5 years?

Costs and pricing

1. What is the cost history and structure of the firm's product?
2. What information is obtainable on competitors' cost structures?

3. Does the firm have any advantages in production costs over the competitors?

4. Does the firm have any advantages in marketing costs over the competitors?

5. Is a standard cost system in use for projecting profits?

6. Does the firm have any advantages in procurement costs over the competitors?

7. How do R & D expenditure and results compare with competitors?

8. How is the quoted price for an order calculated (e.g., individually standard list prices and discounts; individually for large orders)?

9. What discount structure does the firm and its competitors operate—e.g., bulk, seasonal, type of customer (e.g., OEM, contractor, wholesaler, end-user), retrospective, other?

10. What has been the annual average change in price of the firm's and competitors' products/services over the last 5 years?

11. What percentage of the overall price change over the last 5 years has been due to product/service modifications?

12. When was the firm's and competitors' last price change?

13. What were the reasons?

14. How does the firm's price compare with competitors'? What accounts for this similarity/difference?

15. Do any of the products/services under review act as 'loss leaders' to the total range? If so, which?

16. Are variances from list price controlled by the appropriate managers?

17. Are special pricing arrangements, promotional prices and 'deals' reported as variance from list prices?

18. Are prices compared country to country?

19. Are competitive pricing analyses and rationales available explaining differences?

20. Are there historical records on product pricing including percentage increases and decreases?

The product

1. What are the major and subsidiary uses for the firm's product?

2. How do the major uses for the firm's product compare with the major uses for competitors' products?

3. What is the width of the firm's range?

4. What is the depth of the firm's range?

5. Under what conditions are the firm's products used?

6. Is the product incorporated into any other products and is it identifiable when incorporated?

7. What is the extent of these additional uses?

8. What is the idealized 'profile' for a product of the type being marketed?

9. How far does the firm's product accord with the users' idealized conception of the product?

10. What are the product's unique qualities?

11. What are the product's 'plusses'?

12. What are its weaknesses?

13. How does the product differ from
    - 10 years ago?
    - 5 years ago?
    - last year?
14. What changes have been made in the product since its introduction?
15. What were the reasons for changes?
16. What technical changes have occurred in the processes in which the product is used?
17. Have ranges been extended or reduced since they were introduced?
18. What were the reasons for range changes?
19. What support do other products/services give the main product (e.g., extends range, production, and procurement advantages purchased by the same buyers)?
20. What is the reputation of the firm's product in its principal applications?
21. What changes in materials, products, processes, or end-use products are likely to limit or increase demand for the firm's product?
22. How do proposed modifications in product or product range measure up to market demand and trends?
23. What is the percentage of the firm's and competitors' sales broken down by quality range?
    - High
    - Medium
    - Low
24. What is the image of the product?
25. What is the quality spread?
    - Great
    - Small
26. How far beyond the buyer is the product known in the user firm and how far is it associated with the supplier's name?
27. How far can special orders be handled or undertaken?
28. How strong are patents?
29. Can raw material purchases be bulked?
30. What standards exist for the product, and does the product conform to them?
31. What new standards are likely to be adopted?
32. What guarantees are offered and what is guarantee claim record?
33. Is it possible to achieve a high 'break cost'?

Services[1]

1. What design services are required?
   - Physical planning
   - Pre-sale service and advice
   - Prototype fabrication
   - Equipment design and checking
   - Facilities advice
   - Packaging advice

1. This group also comprises some of List 3, 'The service element in marketing', Appendix 3A.

2. What pre-start-up services are required?
   - Assembly
   - Installation
   - Engineering and inspection and testing
3. What negotiation services are required?
   - Resolving complaints
   - Warranty adjustments including exchange of product
   - Liaison between customers and production department
4. What education services are required?
   - Guidance on application use and adaptation of products to customers' needs
   - On-site demonstration, instructions, training, and in-plant lectures
   - Handling and safety advice
   - Library service
   - Technical literature
   - General industrial advice
5. What visiting services are required?
   - General and specific purpose visits to customer's plants
   - Customer visits to service and production departments
6. What maintenance and repair services are required?
   - Periodic testing and adjustment
   - Cleaning and repairing
   - Rehabilitation and reconditioning
   Is loan equipment required?
7. What product adaptation services are required?
   - Modifications
   - Applications research
8. What emergency assistance is required?
9. What standby facilities for emergency and peak-load periods are required?

Marketing research

1. How does marketing research expenditure compare with competitors'?
2. What marketing research has been accomplished in home and export markets?
3. How effective has it been?
4. How efficient are the firm's information sources?
5. How comprehensive are the firm's statistical data?
6. Which methods of marketing research have been found to be most effective?
7. What experimentation in marketing research is taking place?
8. In what circumstances is the use of independent agencies preferred to the firm's own research?
9. What methods exist for obtaining product intelligence?

Overseas markets[1]

1. Have all possible overseas markets been evaluated? (See Appendix 5A.)
2. What criteria will be used to decide on the attractiveness of a market?
3. What official assistance is available for (a) provision of information on individual markets? (b) finance for research? (c) market entry? (d) market consolidation?

1. This group is a summary of List 5, 'Export marketing'.

4. Can earnings be remitted to the exporting country?

5. How narrowly based is the economy and what are trading conditions for principal exports?

6. What is the local taxation position on:
   - Products?
   - Profits?
   - Labour?
   - Turnover?

7. What is the import duty for each of the main exporting countries?

8. Do quotas or licensing arrangements exist?

9. Are local producers protected?

10. Do specific countries and/or firms have official or unofficial preferences in seeking supplying countries?

11. What are local charges?
    - Dock dues
    - Landing charges
    - Clearance charges
    - Weighing and measuring
    - Shipping agents
    - Local transport
    - Certification

12. What production is taking place under licence from foreign competitors?

13. What development schemes are taking place or are planned that will affect demand for the product and business conditions in general?

14. What physical conditions call for product and packaging modifications?

15. What type of sales organization will be required for the territory (e.g., own salesmen, distributor, agent trading company, joint venture, etc.)?

16. What criteria will be used to select and evaluate the sales organization appointed?

17. How will distributors/agents, etc., be remunerated?

18. What form of contract will be used (exclusivity, provision of services, minimum stock levels, extent of marketing effort, etc.)?

19. What contribution will the firm make (sales visits, sales aids, exhibitions, advertising, point of sale, etc.)?

New products

1. What industries will use the new product?

2. Has the product a potential market among institutional and government users?

3. Will the new product round out the firm's lines?

4. How will the new full line compare with those of competitors?

5. Will the new product fill idle time of plant and equipment?

6. Will the new product contribute to long-term growth and security of the business?

7. Will the new product contribute to a lessening of the effects of business cycles?

8. Will the new product put excess capital to work?

9. Will the new product be accepted because it satisfies some need and sells at a price prospective buyers will pay?

10. Will the new product have to penetrate an already developed field?

11. Does the new product offer some important competitive advantages in a developed field?
12. Will the new product, even without competitive superiority, penetrate a developed field by virtue of the firm's reputation or other factors?
13. Will marketing agreements, franchises, etc., in any way limit production, sales, or the use of the product?
14. Is there any element in pricing policy or trade practice that may be a violation of law or accepted trade practice?
15. Are buyers of the new product accustomed to purchasing ahead of need, or do they order for immediate delivery?
16. What is the structure of the raw and processed material and equipment supply industries for the manufacture of the new product?
17. How secure are material and components supplies?
18. What stocks of materials and components are necessary and usual?
19. What substitutes are available?
20. How deep-seated are existing loyalties and how receptive are buyers to new products?
21. What are user preferences in relation to distributive channels and methods for the products of the new product type?
22. What standards (official or unofficial) exist or are likely to be adopted?
23. Can 'top-out' signs be identified?
24. Are there any influences or specifiers involved in purchase decision (e.g., consultants, contractors, etc.)?

Competitive climate

1. Which firms make competitive products?
2. What are their respective market shares?
3. How firmly entrenched are competitors?
4. What specific advantages do the main competitors have?
   - Geographical
   - Industrial
   - Size
   - Related products
   - Commercial and industrial associations and liaisons
   - Protection—official and unofficial
   - Tied-in distributor network
   - Image
   - Approvals
5. What is the reputation of the leading competitors?
6. What methods of distribution are used?
7. Are franchises used?
8. What is their sales structure?
9. What sales promotion techniques are used?
10. What services do competitors offer?
11. What are the usual credit and discount practises?

12. What guarantees are offered?
13. What is the firm's and competitors' policy in relation to the use of technical and non-technical salesmen?
14. What is the sales history of the firm's and competitors' technical and non-technical salesmen?
15. What is the extent of competitors' product research and development?
16. What is the quality of personnel and management?
17. What is the manufacturing potential of principal competitors?
18. What are competitors' appropriations for advertising and sales promotion generally?
19. Are changes in materials or methods likely to increase present competitors' sales?
20. What proportion of competitors' output is sold for export?
21. Which are their principal export markets?
22. What is the extent of competitors' marketing research?
23. What is the image of competitive firms?
24. Have competitive firms built in a 'break cost' element?
25. Do competitors offer loan equipment?
26. What is the extent of manufacturing for private brands?

Competitive prices

1. How does gross price compare with strictly comparable products?
2. How does net price compare with strictly comparable products?
3. How does gross price compare with substitute products?
4. How does net price compare with substitute products?
5. How does the firm's discount structure compare with competitors'?
6. What hidden discounts are offered by competitors?
7. What other 'off-setting against price' factors exist?
8. What is the price history of the most popular unit of sale?
9. What is the price history of the least popular unit of sale?
10. How do distributor margins allowed compare with those granted by competitors?
11. How do distributors' profits actually obtained compare with those obtained on competitors' products?
12. What are the reasons for fluctuations in price?
13. Is price used as part of competitors' marketing strategy?
14. How do spares/service/installation/maintenance/technical advisory charges compare with those of competitors?
15. Is price-fixing practised?
16. How sensitive is the market to price changes?

Competitive processes

1. Do processes not incorporating or using the product offer significant cost advantages?

2. Do processes not incorporating or using the product offer significant production advantages?

3. What technological developments are occurring or being explored which may lead to product obsolescence in particular processes?

4. What technological developments are occurring or being explored which may lead to new demands for the product in new processes using or incorporating them?

5. What is the reputation and record of success of processes not using the product?

6. What is the reputation and record of success of processes using the product?

7. What is the reputation of the firm's product in its principal applications?

Competitive products

1. How do competitive products closely similar in characteristics compare?

2. How do competitive products, dissimilar but substitutable for the firm's product, compare?

3. What are competitive products' 'plusses'?

4. What additional products in competitors' ranges give them sales advantages?

5. What sales advantages does availability of products in depth give competitors?

6. To what extent do unrelated products or processes compete with the new products?

7. How far do competitors' products accord with the idealized 'profile' for the product?

8. What is the reputation of competing products?

9. How does the product compare on:
   - Price?
   - Quality?
   - Performance?
   - Finish, design?
   - Length of service?
   - Packaging or methods of packing?
   - Guarantees?
   - Other characteristics?

10. What are bases of the purchasing decision in relation to competitive products?
    - Price
    - Technical specification
    - Other physical characteristics
    - Delivery and services
    - Packaging or packing method
    - Supporting services provided
    - Company's reputation and guarantees
    - Brand or product reputation
    - Reciprocal trade agreements
    - Company affiliations
    - Personal relationships
    - Approvals

11. What stocks are normally held?
    - At the plant?
    - By distributors?
    - By users?

12. What is the history and cause of sales fluctuations over the last few years?

13. What is the history of firm or brand leadership over the last few years, and what were the reasons for changes?

14. Under what manufacturing conditions are competitive products used?

15. How far beyond the buyer are competitive products known in the user firms, and how far are they associated with competitors by name?

16. What uses do the products have other than those promoted?

17. To what extent are these uses practised?

18. What changes have competitors made in their products since their introduction?

19. What were the reasons for changes in products?

20. Have ranges been extended or reduced since they were introduced?

21. What were the reasons for range changes?

22. How strong are patents?

23. How closely do competitors' products conform to official and unofficial standards?

Demand

1. What is the demand history for the product?

2. How well is demand met by current suppliers?

3. What are the limitations to demand?
   - Technical characteristics
   - Availability of purchasing power
   - Availability of products
   - Substitutions
   - Obsolescence
   - Fashion
   - Seasonal or physical factors
   - Price
   - Availability of services

4. How do the firm's products fit within acceptable style/quality price range?

5. Are the product characteristics acceptable to the majority of purchasers?

6. How does demand vary between the various strata of the market?
   - Industrial
   - Geographical
   - By size of firm
   - In specific uses

7. What conditions in the end-user markets are affecting demand?

8. How many potential users are there of the product in terms of:
   - Industries?
   - Firms?
   - Geographical areas?
   - In specific uses?
   - By specific benefits?

9. What is the average rate of consumption?
   - By industry?
   - By size of firm?
   - By process?
   - By season?
   - In specific uses?

10. What factors affect consumption rate?
11. What characteristics identify the largest customers?
12. What characteristics identify the smallest customers?
13. How stable would demand be in time of depression?
14. How stable would demand be in time of war?
15. What requirements are there for hire or lease facilities and loan equipment?

User attitudes and behaviour

1. What are the decision-forming factors in purchasing, broken down by
   - Industry?
   - Size of firm?
   - Geographical areas?
   - Job function of buyers?
   - Season?
2. What subjective factors are important in buying decisions?
3. Who comprise the decision-making unit in customer firms?
4. What is the usual status and job definition of buyers of the firm's and competitive products?
5. How far is buying a function of a committee?
6. What is the usual method of negotiating orders and contracts?
7. What inter-personal factors exist affecting sales by the firm and by competitors?
8. What preferences exist among users for specific methods of selling and sales promotion?
9. What is the frequency or periodicity of purchase?
10. What is the extent of user knowledge of the firm's products?
11. What is the extent of user knowledge of identical competitive products?
12. What is the extent of user knowledge of competitive substitute products?
13. What is the extent of misuse of the product?
14. How does the user judge the end of the useful life of the product?
15. How do decisions concerning the end of the useful life of the product vary between industries and firms?
16. Are the criteria for judging the end of the useful life of the firm's products the same as those applied to competitors' products?
17. Does buying responsibility change at discrete points, which may alter the product's acceptability within an industrial firm?
18. What size of orders should be expected, broken down by
   - Industry?
   - Size of firm?
   - Geographical location?
   - Job definition and status of buyers?
19. What are the history of and the reasons for lost orders?
20. What are the history of and reasons for cancelled orders?
21. How postponable is purchasing?
22. What commercial conditions are required?

23. What requirements exist for products to be supplied under 'own brand'?
24. Have user preference distributions been studied?
25. What is the total number of firms or installations that could feasibly utilize the products/services?
26. Do users buy direct or through other channels (e.g., distributors, contractors)?
27. What lead times do users generally require?
28. Are there any technical or commercial links between competitors and customers that influence the market?

Governmental factors

1. What is the current tax structure on
   - The product?
   - The end products?
2. What is the history of taxation of the product and end products?
3. What is the import duty?
4. What restrictions on imports exist?
5. What restrictions are imposed on credit terms?
6. What would be the effect of tax changes on demand?
7. What is the position in relation to protection, subsidies, and support prices?
8. What is the government attitude to price agreements and restrictive practices?
9. What legislation exists on safety, quality control, and weights and measures?
10. What is the extent of government participation in purchasing?
11. What is the role of international agencies?
12. What governmental aid schemes exist—e.g., subsidies, protection, loans, credit, holidays, etc.?

Image[1]

1. What is the industry image reference?
2. How does the firm's image compare with industry image?
3. How far does the industry image affect the firm's and its competitors' image?
4. To what extent is the industry image compared with the image of other industries?
5. How do the competitive firms' images compare?
6. What is the product or service image of the firm and its competitors?
7. What is the image of the firm and competitive supporting services?
8. What is the image of the firm's and competitors' personnel—sales, administrative, technical, service?
9. What is the image of the firm's and competitors' premises?
10. How do the images vary between different classifications of customer?
    - Regular
    - Sporadic
    - Single transactions
    - Discontinued customers
    - Failed quotations
    - No contact

1. This group encapsulates List 21, 'Images and perceptions'.

11. How far are the images uncovered based on
    - Direct experience?
    - Known by reputation?
    - Heard of by name?
12. What is the 'mirror' image?
13. What is the 'wish' image?
14. Has the 'optimum' image been identified?
15. Is there any image variation within the DMUs?
16. What factors are influencing image perception?

Marketing systems audit

1. Are sales and margins of specific product and product group units reported regularly?
2. Do sales/margins reports go to the correct managers?
3. Are product line contribution reports produced regularly?
4. Do managers receive
    - Price reviews?
    - Cost analysis?
    - Promotions analysis?
    - Product additions?
    - Product deletions?
    - Product line item count growth?
5. Are annual sales contracts reviewed regularly to determine the impact of cost changes?
6. Are receivables monitored by marketing management?
7. Are credits/returns corrected and detailed on sales and margin reports?
8. Are credits and returns monitored according to product and product lines? Reason? Authorized by management?
9. Is there a formalized credit rating system?
10. Is the credit rating of customers periodically reviewed?
11. Are detailed inventory reports available to appropriate marketing management?
12. Is inventory analysed in terms of on-going, obsolete, and related to short-term forecast sales?
13. Is there a formal marketing plan, by product line?
14. Do all relevant managers have copies of marketing plans?
15. Is the marketing plan regularly used by managers?
16. Does the senior marketing manager regularly review progress against plan with responsible manager?
17. Are objectives reviewed as to their relevance on the year's progress?

Appendix 6B(i). Choosing the right research organization

The following check list may be helpful in selecting the research organization best suited to particular needs. It covers the salient points on which a firm should satisfy itself in short-listing and selecting a marketing research company to conduct a project. It is rarely helpful to consider more than three companies in detail.

A rating method applied to each factor is usually most effective if the number of points can be limited. A suggestion is:

Very good	+2
Good	+1
Average	0
Poor	−1
Very poor	−2

However, not all the factors are of equal importance and will require weighting to be sure that each one considered is given its due significance; for example, in most circumstances, numbers of full-time professional staff will be less important than research capability in the area under consideration. If both are very good (i.e., +2 each), the factor total would be 4. This would not make the needed distinction. By weighting 'number of full-time professional staff' by 1 and 'research capability in the subject' by 2, a distinction is achieved which recognizes the importance of the second factor ('numbers of full-time professional staff' $+2 \times 1 = +2$; 'capability in area researched' $+2 \times 2 = +4$).

A suggested weighting is:

3	Very important
2	Important
1	Of moderate significance

The ratings and weightings system is similar to that in the market selection procedure in List 5, 'Export marketing', Appendix 5A.

Appendix 6B(ii).   Points to be evaluated

The weightings given are suggestions only but will be applicable for the majority of firms without internal marketing research and who are seeking outside services.

Company A Name...

Company B Name...

Company C Name...

	Suggested weighting	Company A	Company B	Company C
A Reputation				
1. Reputation of the firm in general	3			
2. Reputation of firm in our industry or industry to be investigated	2			
3. Reputation of individual members of firm	1			
4. Agency's clients' evaluation of their ability and capability	2			
5. Agency's clients in our own fields' evaluation of their ability and capability	2			
6. Professional and other non-commercial bodies' approval	2			
7. Number and types of the agency's clients in our own field	1			
8. Financial strength	2			
B Organization				
1. Links with other organizations	2			
2. Method of overseas operation	2			
3. Directors' other interests	2			
4. Extent of use of external advisers or associates	2			
5. Terms of business (payment method, etc.)	1			
TOTAL c/f				

	Suggested weighting	Company A	Company B	Company C
TOTAL b/f				
C Capability and experience				
1. Length of time established	1			
2. Degree of specialization in industrial marketing research	3			
3. Degree of specialization in our field or the field to be investigated	2			
4. Degree of specialization in techniques	1			
5. Conformity of completed projects with our special interests	1			
6. Links with learned institutions and/or universities	2			
7. Understanding of problem	3			
8. Unambiguous research design—clarity and detail	3			
D Qualifications and proof of professional ability				
1. Types of research staff used and conformity to our requirements	3			
2. Qualifications of research staff	3			
3. Extent of repeat business	2			
4. Fields in which technical expertise is claimed	2			
5. Any client recommendations or references	2			
6. Staff membership of professional organizations and societies	1			
E Evidence of professional leadership				
1. Publications	1			
2. Academic contributions	1			
3. New technique developments	2			
4. Non-sponsored research into techniques and practices	2			
5. Agency's contribution to state of the art of industrial marketing research	1			
TOTAL c/f				

74

	Suggested weighting	Company A	Company B	Company C
TOTAL b/f				
F Resources				
(i) *Staff*				
Number of full-time qualified professional staff	1			
Number of part-time professional staff	2			
Number of support staff	2			
Interview force (permanent)	3			
Interview force (part-time)	2			
(ii) *Directors*				
Qualifications and experience in industrial market research	3			
Involvement in preparing projects	2			
Involvement in undertaking projects	1			
Involvement in presentation of projects and follow-up	2			
Extent of directorial responsibility for projects	3			
(iii) *Premises*				
Location	1			
Size	2			
Adequacy and conditions	2			
Equipment	1			
TOTAL				

Appendix 6C. Evaluating research[2]

- What was the research attempting to achieve?
- How did the research attempt to achieve what it set out to do?
- Is there a sufficient n imber of facts and are they satisfactorily validated?
- Was the methodology correct?
- Did the research succeed or fail in its objectives?
- How 'hedged' was the reporting?
- What degree of confidence can be placed on the results?
- How far do the final results depart from the agreed research design?
- Are the reasons for any departures valid?
- Could they have been foreseen before the research began?
- Was the researcher suitably qualified and experienced to carry out the project? How much reliance can be placed on his judgement?
- Is the report intended to inform? Does it do this?
- How far is the report an explanation or a plea? Are these justified?
- Has the research coverage been adequate?
- Have all secondary sources of information been tapped?
- Is the research taken to the most recent date possible?
- Is the project logical, complete, and well-designed?
- Are the conclusions justified by the facts?
- Are the recommendations reasonable and do they take account of internal factors?
- Is the reasoning correct and without fallacies?

2. Aubrey Wilson, *The Assessment of Industrial Markets*, Associated Business Programmes, London, 1973, pp. 332–3.

List 7. Market size and structure

Introduction

The size and configuration of a market are almost invariably the first questions asked in either appraising an existing market or product or considering new products or marketing, and certainly these are highly important factors in the internal marketing audit. However, market size and structure are not necessarily the most important issues. For example, the size of the market for digital multimeters could be described as 'big enough', but for one consumer electronics manufacturer the critical factor for success was his need for acceptance as a committed supplier of professional instruments rather than as a firm selling DIY products through retail chains.

Having said that, however, it would be an odd marketing audit that did not attempt to make some estimate of its current and potential market and then compare the company's performance with the position as revealed. A firm's markets are as much part of its resources as are the factory, offices, machinery, staff, and know-how.

In basing market action on assessments, it is necessary to have a realistic view as to their validity. Where market estimates and their breakdowns are not derived from research, official, or trade association statistics, they tend to take on the aspects of the children's game of Chinese Whispers. They become distorted and exaggerated, and then hallowed by repetition. Great care should be taken in arriving at an estimate to examine the facts and if possible the sources that lead to the conclusions drawn. It is crucial to tap all useful sources within the company (see List 4, 'Company performance', and List 6, 'Marketing information: systems and use') and to check salesmen's reports with other personnel whose performance is not judged by the apparent market size and their share of it.

There is no real substitute for research, but it is recognized that for the marketing audit purpose it may not be cost-effective. Therefore best judgement, perhaps compiled on a Delphi basis, must substitute, but the market auditor should always be aware of possible deficiencies in the estimates and should attempt to place some degree of confidence on each one.

The answer to Question 7.1 is of course the uptake, not the production, of the product/service in the country under review. To arrive at this figure it is necessary to add imports to domestic production and deduct exports to obtain the net market figure. These amendments should not be omitted.

It will be found that this list gives some very clear guidelines as to actions required in specific market situations. The second question, for example, directs attention to a hidden trap in many markets. Research and other methods of market assessment often fail to take account of the difference between the uptake of a product or service and that which is bought in the open market. For example, one section of the hydraulic cylinder market is reduced from £25.7 million to an available market of a mere £6.0 million when business never available to an outside supplier is removed.[1] That is not to say that in-fed markets cannot be successfully penetrated, only that they set the marketer a particularly difficult task that is best not attempted if there are other 'softer' markets to go for.

Question 7.3 looks at market share. It is always important to ask 'share of what?' By way of an example, and to show how misleading market share can be as an indication of performance, it is worth quoting the case of an anti-asthma drug. In this £5 million market one firm had a 20 per cent share of the market but 30 per cent in terms of prescriptions issued. However, this represented the prescribing of only 18 per cent of all doctors, although 40 per cent of sufferers were using the brand. The study by Simon Marjaro[2] pointed out 30 per cent of all prescriptions issued for anti-asthma drugs of this category was good news but only 18 per cent of doctors prescribing was bad news. These four different ways of looking at market share in this case illustrate how deceptive such figures might be unless the key question, 'share of what?' is answered first.

Questions 7.18–7.20 are best dealt with as a vulnerability analysis which is explained in the Introduction to List 1, 'Marketing strategy and planning'.

A caveat is needed concerning competition, although this will be dealt with in great depth in List 17, 'Competitive climate'. Competition should not be judged too narrowly. It is not just directly comparable products/services, but must include different products/services that will achieve the same end or benefits for the user. Here products and services can compete head-on. Laundry versus disposable work wear, contract cleaners versus cleaning equipment. Similarly, in identifying competitors it is as well to include significant importers or distributors, or, in the case of distributor competitors, direct trading manufacturers.

The early questions on the current market, both as it is now constituted and as the 'fairy tale' absolute total market (if everyone who could use the product/service actually used it), point to a marketing direction and to activities that also involve other parts of the firm. A simple question, all too often overlooked, as to what changes in the product/service ranges offered and commercial terms, etc., would open up new segments, is formulated in 7.25. There is an example of a spring balancer used for holding spot welding guns. Looking at it not as an ancillary for a machine tool, but as a piece of equipment that permitted something to be turned through 360 degrees and lifted or lowered and then left in the chosen attitude, it was found there were applications in meat preparation, tanneries, and very many craft industries. The modification to the balancer was minor, the new market openings huge.

The positioning map in the last question is a valuable exercise which will often prove if there really is a highly priced competitive market. It will frequently be found that, despite reports (usually the salesmen's) that the market is cut-throat, the bulk of the market is held by firms whose price is relatively high. In open steel flooring, for example, well over 60 per cent of the market is in the hands of firms whose price is in the high quartile, and this despite the existence of low-price flooring.

This check list links with a number of previous and later ones. In particular, the marketing auditor is advised to use the questions completed in List 4, 'Company performance' (particularly Questions 4.5, 4.8, 4.9, 4.10, and 4.15), and List 5, 'Export marketing', Questions 5.1 and 5.3 for comparison purposes.

1. Aubrey Wilson and Bryan Atkin, 'Exorcising the ghosts in marketing', *Harvard Business Review*, Cambridge Mass., September/October 1976.
2. Simon Marjaro, 'Market share: deception or diagnosis', *Marketing*, London, March 1977.

7.1 What is the size of the total market for our product/service as presently used? (See Introduction and compare answer with List 4, 'Company performance', Questions 4.3–4.5 and List 16, 'User industries', Question 16.1.)

7.2 How much of the market is subject to in-feeding and reciprocal trading arrangements? (See Introduction and List 16, 'User industries', Question 16.32.)

7.3 What is our market share? (See Introduction.)

7.4 What is the basis for acceptance of the figures, and what degree of accuracy can we ascribe to them?

7.5 What would the market be if our product/service were to be used in all possible applications? (See answer to List 8, 'Future market', Question 8.22.)

7.6 What are the total number of establishments who could use our product/service in its present application?

7.7 What are the total number of establishments who could use our product/service if it were purchased for all possible applications? (This answer will be required again in List 16, 'User industries', Question 16.7.)

7.8 How many of these establishments are currently customers?

7.9 How many of these establishments are regularly contacted?

7.10 Breakdown of the total market by:

- End use or application
- OEM industries
- Products
- Dimensions
- Price
- Handling method
- Territory or region
- Imports/exports
- Retrofit
- Replacement
- Through distributors
- Quality range
- Size of orders
- Frequency of orders
- Seasonal
- Performance requirements

(See answer in List 2, 'Product/service range', Question 2.2, List 4, 'Company performance', Question 4.10, and List 16, 'User industries', Question 16.1.)

7.11 Breakdown of market by individual salesmen or agents. (See answer in List 4, 'Company performance', Question 4.8.) (Note that sales into territory does not necessarily equate with salesmen or agent performance.)

7.12 What are our main domestic and foreign direct competitors?

7.13 Who are the main indirect competitors? (See Introduction.)

7.14 Assessment of our competitors' market share. What reliability can we place on this estimate? (See Introduction; this information will also be needed for List 17, 'Competitive climate', Question 17.3.)

7.15 How have these varied over the last three to five years?

7.16 How can we account for competitor market share and variations? (This information will also be needed for List 17, 'Competitive climate', Question 17.5.)

7.17 How durable is the market? (The answer to this and questions 7.18–7.26 should align with List 16, 'User industries', Question 16.37.)

7.18 What factors threaten the market? (See List 1, 'Marketing strategy and planning', Introduction, on vulnerability analysis in relation to this and the next two questions.)

7.19 What would the impact of these threats be on the firm and the market? (This information will be needed for List 8, 'Future market', Question 8.9.)

7.20 What is the likelihood of the threats occurring?

7.21 What control and influence do we have over the threats?

7.22 What steps can be taken to avert the threat and on what time scale?

7.23 What factors will stimulate the market?

7.24 What actions can we take to encourage any favourable trends?

7.25 What changes in product/service, the ranges offered, commercial terms, and other operational aspects would widen the market? (See Introduction and compare answers with Question 7.5 and List 16, 'User industries', Question 16.6.)

7.26 How feasible are such changes?

7.27 On what information are our answers to 7.25 and 7.26 based?

7.28 How reliable and recent is it?

7.29 What is the extent of own uptake of the specified products/services? (See the answer to List 4, 'Company performance', Question 4.15.)

7.30 What are the extent of our sales to suppliers on a reciprocal trading basis? (Compare answer with Question 7.2.)

7.31 Do we want to increase/decrease either or own uptake or reciprocal trading?

7.32 How much business stems from organizations or individuals who influence/advise on the use of products/services (e.g., consultants, architects, accountants)? (See List 2, 'Product/service range', Questions 2.19 and 2.21, and List 5, 'Export marketing', Questions 5.42 and 5.43.)

7.33 If the market is cyclical, what is the periodicity? What causes it?

7.34 How great are sales variations between peaks and troughs?

7.35 Are there any anti-cyclical products/services in our range under consideration or being sought?

7.36 Can we develop anti-cyclical products or services? (See List 15, 'Introducing new products/services', Question 15.24.)

7.37 Relate market share to price on the positioning map. (See Introduction and cross-reference with the positioning maps in List 16, 'User industries', Question 16.50, and List 20, 'Pricing', Question 20.3.)

(The auditor should indicate on the vertical scale either an accurate or perceived price level of his own and major competitors' prices and on the horizontal scale the actual or estimated market shares. This will clearly indicate the price–market share relationship.)

List 8. Future market

Introduction

'The only good thing about the future', said Herman Khan, 'is that it comes one day at a time.' True as this may be, the nature of business demands that the future be under constant review and, equally, that plans for the future also be under constant review and always contain a contingency element. Markets are perhaps one of the most hazardous of all areas to forecast—the variables being as great as in any other discipline and the movements perhaps more volatile and unpredictable than most. Nevertheless, the difficulty of the task is not a reason for not undertaking it in a methodical manner and applying best judgement to situations that defy stricter analysis.

Forecasting, more than any other aspect of marketing audits, requires detailed, recent, and accurate information, and much that is included in List 6, 'Marketing information: systems and use', is directed to producing a relatively high confidence level in prognostications.

A great deal of the raw data required for forecasting can be obtained from many official, semi-official and unofficial sources, specialist organizations such as the Henley Centre, and data books of various types. This applies to both the UK and overseas territories. Most commercial or specialist libraries can provide a useful bibliography, but the auditor must again be warned of getting diverted in information-gathering and sophisticated analytical techniques at the expense of the interpretation.

For marketing audit purposes qualitative assessment are as important as numerical precision, and the views of those interfacing with the market and competitors is as significant a contribution as industry output data.

It is necessary in dealing with forecasting for the marketing auditor to make his own decision as to what data give a reliable guide to future requirements. The questions provide a framework within which, and from which, the final lists can be developed.

For forecasts to be useful they require constant monitoring. As the events of the last two decades have shown, the hypotheses on which a medium term forecast is based is highly unlikely to be valid through the period. It is only necessary to look at energy prices in 1972 and 1981, unemployment rates in 1975 and 1982 or Iran as a market in 1976 and 1980 to see how violently different forecasts can be from the ultimate reality. There is only one possible approach to adopt to avoid the trap. This is to state clearly the hypotheses upon which a forecast is based and to have a series of contingency plans which can be initiated if there is a significant variation in the forecast as a result of a change in the factors on which it was based. That is not to say that the market plan should be adjusted for every variation that occurs; a sensible judgement will tell the marketing auditor when there must be a touch on the tiller or when a new course must be navigated.

82

The most useful first step is to decide which business indicators are significant. For most firms the major economic indicators are useful only in a macro-sense and the individual company requires micro-forecasting. There are, however, well accepted and thoroughly reliable economic lead–lag indicators which can be applied to the individual firm; and, oddly enough, there are also corporate indicators that can be used to forecast national economic trends. It is well known that employment agency services feel the shock waves of recession long before any official statistics reveal the position. An early task for the auditor is to identify those external lead–lag indicators which have a meaning for the firm and the internal ones which historically lead to a given situation. The answers to question 8.1 for perhaps the more fortunate company may be a wholly reliable forecast in themselves. For the less closely correlated situations they will make a significant contribution to the forecast.

However, as with other types of information, it is important to emphasize again that receiving data for forecasting or the actual forecasts themselves are not a substitute for action. Questions 8.3 and 8.4 are a very adequate test as to whether information perhaps laboriously and expensively gathered is in fact fully utilized.

Segmentation already referred to in List 1, 'Marketing strategy and planning', Question 1.17, List 2, 'Product/service range', Question 2.2, and List 4, 'Company performance', Question 4.4, takes on yet another significance if any part of the market is likely to grow or decline faster than others. The danger of regarding a market that is in fact the aggregate of a number of disparate parts as homogeneous is obvious. Question 8.6 breaks down global into the segment expectations.

The market for package steam generators may have an overall growth rate of 10 per cent, but the hospital sector could show nil growth, while hotels demand might well be in excess of 16 per cent. This illustrates the importance of Question 8.6.

This leads to another danger in forecasting, which Question 8.20 touches on: the failure to distinguish between what the market would like and what it has the resources to purchase. A number of major electronic firms are still licking their wounds over sophisticated teaching laboratories which every educational establishment in the world would like to possess but few can afford to buy. The research showed a demand but failed to show a major lack of resource to fulfil the requirement.[1]

Attention is drawn to Question 8.23 for the many firms whose products, or indeed marketing methods, might be favourably or adversely effected by legislation. If increasing public pressure for higher standards of restaurant hygiene leads to greater regulation and control, then a demand will be engendered not only for cleaning equipment and services, but also for products and materials that are easier to maintain or handle. The intention expressed by successive governments to prevent the professions from continuing their restrictive practices on advertising, if enacted, could create new demand for advertising agency services. However, legislation proposed or even enacted is still fraught with dangers for forecasting purposes. The EEC law on tachometers which was passed several years ago should have created a demand for tachometers, but this has been very considerably delayed because of opposition by the transport drivers and their unions. There is a lesson here: proposed legislation may not in fact reach the statute books; and when it does, it may not be implemented.

Forecasting the future without using the information in some practical way is an interesting but, on its own, substantially useless exercise. The whole point of forecasting is to be able to make plans to avert threats and to exploit opportunities that arise. The

1. Aubrey Wilson and Bryan Atkin, 'Exorcising ghosts in marketing', *Harvard Business Review*, Cambridge, Mass., September/October 1976.

vulnerability analysis method set out in the Introduction to List 1, 'Marketing strategy and planning', will be found to be a very useful tool for micro-forecasting.

It is obvious, of course, that the company's marketing can have a strong influence on the way a market will go. The impact of any marketing plans ought to be considered in the forecast. At the same time, it is as well to ensure that the forecast does not become a self-fulfilling prophecy. Both factors will be considered automatically in answering Question 8.31.

It is recognized the check list that follows has many shortcomings. This one, more than most others, is intended to give starting torque to the forecasters and is by no means the last word on the subject.

8.1 Which economic/industry/social (lead–lag) indicators have a significance for us? (This question will have been answered in List 6, 'Marketing information: systems and use', Question 6.35.)

8.2 Who in our organization receives them?

8.3 What procedures are followed in their use?

8.4 What actions have been taken in the past as a result of using market forecasts?

8.5 Estimate the annual average growth rate for the market for our products/services for the next five years. (Distinguish between the market at constant values and any changes that are due to inflation. If possible, 'units' or 'volume' should be used to avoid the problem of high and changing inflation rates.)

8.6 Can the 'global' forecast be broken down into significant segments? (For some suggested segmentation criteria refer to List 2, 'Product/service range, Question 2.2.)

8.7 What hypotheses are the 'global' and segment forecasts based on?

8.8 Indicate any market segment for our products/services growing faster/slower than the total.

8.9 What reasons can we attribute for the growth/decline? (See List 7, 'Market size and structure', Introduction and Questions 7.17, 7.18, 7.19, and 7.23.)

8.10 What opportunities or threats does this imply for us? (See List 7, 'Market size and structure', Questions 7.21 and 7.23.)

8.11 What major technological changes will occur in customers' production and operational methods, equipment, materials used, products/services and in their commercial practices that will affect the demand for our products/services?

8.12 Does our R & D programme reflect these expected changes?

8.13 Do we understand the reasons for any changes?

8.14 What are the implications for us?

8.15 What technical developments in our own and our competitors' products/services production methods/materials used/commercial practices are taking place or expected to take place in the future?

8.16 Do these changes imply a compatibility with the changes referred to in the earlier Questions 8.11 and 8.12?

8.17 Which trends are likely to increase/reduce the number of competitors in the market?

8.18 What new products/services are likely to emerge that may impact on our markets?

8.19 What time span is likely to be involved?

8.20 Is there likely to be any difference in the forecast period between market requirements and its ability to purchase? (See Introduction.)

8.21 Will economic, social, or political changes provide us with new opportunities or create new threats over the next five years? (The answers to this and the previous three questions should be compared with those given in List 15, 'Introducing new products/services', Question 15.31.)

8.22 Are any present non-users likely to take up the product/service in the next five years? (See List 7, 'Market size and structure', Introduction and Question 7.5.)

8.23 Is proposed legislation, domestic, EEC, or international, likely to affect either demand or the structure of the market? (See Introduction.)

8.24 What changes are likely to occur that will restrict or liberalize trading in our major overseas customers? (See answer in List 5, 'Export marketing', to Question 5.16.)

8.25 How will price change over the forecast period (in constant and current price terms)? (See answers in List 20, 'Pricing', Questions 20.33 and 20.34.)

8.26 Which companies (by name) do we think are likely to enter or leave the market over the next five years? (See answer to Question 8.17.)

8.27 What are the reasons?

8.28 What changes in the structure of the market are foreseen (distributors and other intermediaries, buying influences, imports/exports)?

8.29 How accurate have previous forecasts been?

8.30 In what way could we improve accuracy?

8.31 Has the impact of our own, and our competitors', marketing strategies and ambitions been taken into account in arriving at the forecasts? (See Introduction.)

List 9. The sales force

Introduction

'There is no such thing as a bad salesman, only bad sales managers.'

Richard Skinner, marketing director, Reliance Systems Limited

If this is not wholly true, it is uncomfortably close to the position that will be found in many firms. This check list is about selling but must inevitably involve sales management. The marketing auditors may well want to enquire if their sales managers have also asked the questions and if the answers have been used to improve sales performance. Thus the list could have the treble purpose of forming part of the total marketing audit, an audit of sales efficiency, and a sub-audit of sales management effectiveness.

While most check lists, as has been pointed out, have an in-built danger of encouraging the demand for more information and analysis than can profitably be used in an internal marketing audit, this one on selling tempts the compiler to extend the question almost indefinitely, because there is so much that can be asked and so much that can be actioned in the majority of sales organizations. Indeed, this list might well have been sub-titled 'One hundred questions every good sales manager should ask'.

Underlying many of the points is the query whether the reasons that account for present organization and methods are still valid. Too many sales operations are based on history and have not reacted to the rapid changes in market conditions and marketing techniques that typified the last decade.

Throughout the list runs a strong emphasis on examining factors that create salesmen's motivations. Questions such as 9.9–9.11, 9.31, and 9.42 all have strong implications relative to motivation, while Questions 9.12, 9.19, and 9.22–9.25 deal directly with this subject. It is recognized that different things motivate different people, and a mechanistic approach is unlikely to be successful across the whole sales force. Some selling requirements are socially and domestically destructive. The questions seek to draw attention to the fact that, where a salesman is subjected to this type of domestic disruption, there ought to be some compensating factor, an important motivational point that is referred to in some detail later.

Question 9.21 opens up an often neglected aspect of sales force supervision. Commissions often induce price-cutting. Given a 5 per cent commission, a drop in price by the salesmen of 10 per cent means a loss of 0.5 per cent commission but a greater certainty of getting business. (See the formulae in Introduction to List 20, 'Pricing'). It must be asked who would not rather have 4.5 per cent on something than 5 per cent on nothing? Moreover, in getting the order, even at a sub-standard or unprofitable price, it is a fact of life the salesman receives the approval of his superiors, the regard of his peers, and the admiration of his subordinates. No wonder price-cutting is as often the result of salesmen's offers as of buyers' demands.

An interesting illustration of this phenomenon is provided by a firm of electrical insulation material suppliers. Salesmen were given a list price and a minimum price they could negotiate. Prices not unnaturally were invariably nearer the bottom of the range, since the commission differential between top and bottom prices was marginal to the salesman and the chance of the order much higher at the lower price. The company adopted a system of dividing equally with the salesman the incremental price over the set minimum. Within weeks, the average price obtained had risen 35 per cent above the minimum, giving the firm an extra 17.5 per cent and the salesman a substantially higher income.

Question 9.42 focuses on a common—indeed, almost universal—omission in sales management. While it is expected that the salesmen will report to the company, most companies fail to report to the salesman. Such a report can be a very valuable motivation tool. In Appendix 9A will be found a model of a report-back system. It is interesting to note that even the socially and domestically destructive elements in a salesman's schedule, already referred to, are considered in the performance comparison analysis.[1]

While giving salesmen price variation authority will be seen to have its dangers, the other aspect is that it enhances the role and status of the salesmen in the eyes of the customer. This is a trade-off to be considered in making such a decision. Question 9.44 raises the issue.

Question 9.45 may seem a little obscure in its shortened form. There are many ways of selling. Sometimes a firm sells the concept, on the basis that, once this is sold, they will pick up their share of orders. The task of some sales forces is to sell a demonstration, not a product, because they know that a high proportion of demonstrations turn to business. One manufacturer of mixing equipment had not realized that his 80 per cent conversion rate of demonstrations to orders clearly implied that the task was to sell demonstrations, which are easier to arrange than sales. At one time sink-top dishwasher manufacturers would leave the demonstration machine for a week. This led to substantial sales. In some businesses the customer only requires the supplier to put a price on a specification, rather like a barrister and a brief. On the face of it, this leaves little opportunity to apply selling skills. The task is to try and change the customer's approach to his buying. Thus the question calls on the marketing auditor to decide how the product/service is sold and whether there might not be an alternative and better way.

In the Introduction to this book one of the great weaknesses often found in sales forces was illustrated: the difference between available selling days and days actually spent in the field. It cannot be right for personnel with selling skills to be devoting time to tasks that could be done as well, or indeed better, by others, and Questions 9.58–9.64 investigate this point.

An examination of time expenditure of a three-man export sales force based in the UK headquarters of a manufacturer of fast patrol vessels showed that less than 135 days a year were spent in the field—the remainder being justified by 'factory liaison', 'quotation preparation', and other non-selling activities. An increase to a still low figure of 175 days would produce another half-year of selling days. This very simple analysis is one that ought not to be missed by any firm.

This leads straight to the 'cost of call' analysis. Appendix 9B is a suggested model for calculation purposes. While averages obviously disguise great variations, the high cost of a call clearly implies the need for greater sales productivity. The prompts in Question 9.52 identify some methods for consideration, and the importance of doing so may be inherent in the answers to Questions 9.57–9.72.

1. J. B. Maddan, *Motivate Your Salesmen*, MMC Ltd, Calcutta, 1975.

Tangentially, it is worth commenting that in these days of word processors it is possible to mechanize quotation preparation, and this alone can significantly increase salesmen's availability for field, as opposed to office, work.

Question 9.73 is deceptively simple and frequently produces a conditioned response answer. After all, to question whether a salesman knows his territory is criticism of the most severe type. Yet, where a product/service has a multi-industry application—for example, office equipment, cleaning materials, space heating systems, telecoms—virtually every establishment is a potential customer. The salesman must distinguish between worthwhile and other calls, which is not always easy to do, by judging the factory size and operation or the shop from its fascia board. There are however excellent commercial services which can provide data on individual establishments from the name of the buyer or works manager to whether they have a staff canteen or a forklift truck.

The question of customer profiling in 9.79 needs some explanation. This is a simple analytical system for tabulating the major characteristics of good regular customers—e.g., size of company, method of operation, type of activity, form of purchasing organization, or whatever characteristics are appropriate. (List 16, 'User industries', Question 16.9, contains a fuller list of prompts for profiling factors.) This profile is then applied to 'prospect' firms so that those conforming most closely to the 'best customer' profile can be identified and made priority targets.[2] Experience has shown that it is one of the most simple and practical analyses that can be undertaken by a company, which is explained in more detail in the Introduction to List 16, 'User industries'.

Questions 9.85–9.91 can highlight another area of weakness which may be far from obvious. A superbly operating sales force and excellent non-personal promotion can do nothing to obviate incompetent and clumsy processing of enquiries and orders directly received by mail, telephone, or personal calls. The routing of enquiries from the mail room, switchboard, or reception can be the first weak link in a weak chain, followed by the use of low-level clerical staff to handle what might be important actual or potential customers. Getting enquiries or orders wrong, failing to pass messages, telephone back, or write are common errors that do untold damage. The whole system of internal handling of enquiries/orders received direct should always be examined critically, reviewed frequently, and monitored constantly.

The marketing auditor must never lose sight of the fact that the whole company is a selling organism, not just those who have the word 'sales' in their job title. Apart from reception and telephone, which are obvious, the auditor must question whether the accounts department, for example, are pleasant and efficient even when firm in pressing for settlement of overdue accounts; if the service men visiting clients are acceptable to them both in their work and manner. All these aspects and many others are as much part of the sales process as the salesmen's calls.

---

2. A brief description of the system will be found in Aubrey Wilson, *Marketing of Professional Services*, McGraw-Hill, Maidenhead, 1972, pp. 78–9.

9.1 How many salesmen do we have/need?

9.2 What would be the effect on sales of cutting/increasing the sales force?

9.3 How are they organized? By region, by industry/application, by type of customer, by product/service, etc.

9.4 Are the reasons for this form of organization still valid?

9.5 Is the sales force technically qualified in our product or in the customer industries, or not at all?

9.6 What are customer preferences?

9.7 How do we know? (The answer to this and two previous questions will also be required for List 17, 'Competitive climate', Question 17.41.)

9.8 Would meeting the customer preference in this respect be incompatible with our needs?

9.9 What methods of remuneration are we using?

9.10 How does it differ from previous methods?

9.11 Why were the present methods adopted?

9.12 What proof do we have that it provides strong motivation?

9.13 How does our remuneration method compare with competitors?

9.14 Can we justify any differences?

9.15 Have we considered alternative methods?

9.16 What were the criteria for rejection? Are they still valid?

9.17 What other benefits do our salesmen get?

9.18 Are the benefits actually earned, or do they form part of the salary package?

9.19 Would there be a stronger/weaker motivation if benefits were related to performance?

9.20 How are direct orders treated in terms of remuneration and performance appraisal? (Compare with List 12, 'The distributive system', Question 12.36.)

9.21 Does the remuneration system encourage price-cutting by the salesmen? (See Introduction.)

9.22 Would any change in system improve/reduce salesmen's motivation and thus affect performance?

9.23 Rate the motivation of salesmen: high, moderate, low.

9.24 What major factors provide motivation in each salesman?

9.25 Are these emphasized in sales training and induction?

9.26 How are salesmen recruited?

9.27 What is the record of sales force turnover?

9.28 How does it compare with the standard for the industry?

9.29 What is the major cause of losses?

9.30 How far can losses be attributed to poor recruitment criteria and methods, poor induction, inadequate training, supervision, or encouragement?

9.31 What criteria are used for performance evaluation and how frequently is an evaluation made?

9.32 Do the sales force know and understand the criteria used for judging the performance?

9.33 Are the criteria valid in today's conditions?

9.34 What targets do salesmen have? (See List 4, 'Company performance', Question 4.6.)

9.35 How are they devised? (This question will have been answered in List 4, 'Company performance', Question 4.7.)

9.36 Are they reached in agreement with the salesmen?

9.37 If not, is the method of arriving at a target explained to the salesmen?

9.38 How does each salesman perform against target? (Use answers to List 4, 'Company performance', Questions 4.5 and 4.8.)

9.39 How is constant under-performance dealt with?

9.40 Is the method effective?

9.41 What rewards or acknowledgements do salesmen receive for passing targets?

9.42 Is there a report-back system to salesmen so that they can compare their performance with others or with the best and with the firm's progress as a whole? (See Introduction and Appendix 9A.)

9.43 What is the sales platform (features/benefits)? (List 2, 'Product/service range', Introduction, Fig. 2-1 and Questions 2.26–2.28 cross-reference with this point.)

9.44 Do salesmen have authority to vary price? (See List 20, 'Pricing', Question 20.10.)

9.45 Is the product/service sold as a concept, by demonstration, on quotation, or by attribute? (See Introduction.)

9.46 What is the proportion of sales calls to enquiries received?

9.47 What is the proportion of enquiries to quotations?

9.48 What is the proportion of quotations to orders obtained? (The answers to the last two questions should have been given in List 4, 'Company performance', Questions 4.24 and 4.25.)

9.49 How does it vary between salesmen?

9.50 What is the cause of any variation?

9.51 Can favourable variation factors be transferred to other salesmen?

9.52 What steps can we take to eliminate poor performance?

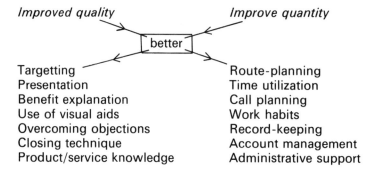

Improved quality   *Improve quantity*

Targetting   Route-planning
Presentation   Time utilization
Benefit explanation   Call planning
Use of visual aids   Work habits
Overcoming objections   Record-keeping
Closing technique   Account management
Product/service knowledge Administrative support

9.53 Do salesmen use an intrinsic or extrinsic approach ('intrinsic' concentrating on the prospect's substantive needs or problems, 'extrinsic' emphasizing the attributes of the firm or product/service without relating it to the customer need)?

9.54 Is the emphasis on the product/service, reputation of the company, or a success they have achieved? Are these approaches suitable and effective? (See List 23, 'Service businesses', Introduction and Question 23.36. Although this refers specifically to service selling, it has direct implications in product selling.)

9.55 What are individual salesmen's performances broken down by industry, application, type or size of company or other breakdowns? (See List 2, 'Product/service range', Question 2.2, which suggests some headings for analysis, and compare answers with List 4, 'Company performance', Questions 4.8 and 4.9.)

9.56 Does this analysis indicate that some salesmen might be better committed to a specialization rather than a territory?

9.57 What is the cost per call? (See Appendix 9B.)

9.58 How many active selling days are there in a year (as compared with total of about 222 in the UK)? (See Introduction.)

9.59 Can the difference between days in the field and days available be justified?

9.60 What steps can be taken to reduce non-selling days?

9.61 Do salesmen prepare their own quotations or tenders?

9.62 Could this work be wholly or partially standardized, simplified, handled by non-selling personnel, or undertaken using computers and/or word processing? (This answer will be required again in List 24, 'Product/service financial information', Question 24.46.)

9.63 What is the average number of calls each day?

9.64 How does this compare between salesmen (allowing for different territorial distribution of customers)?

9.65 How does this compare on an 'all-industry' basis?

9.66 Could the call rate be improved by better call cycle planning? (See Question 9.52.)

9.67 What is the average length of calls?

9.68 Would there be a material improvement in performance if call length were increased/decreased?

9.69 If so, how can the change be achieved?

9.70 What is the average daily mileage?

9.71 Have routings been analysed?

9.72 Are all prospects on routes and off-route known?

9.73 How frequently is the salesman required to spend nights or weekends away from home? (See Introduction and the 'Personal sacrifice' item in the report-back form which is given as Appendix 9A.)

9.74 Is he compensated additionally for this?

9.75 What proportion of total calls are committed to customers? (See List 4, 'Company performance', Questions 4.11 and 4.20.)

9.76 Does the analysis in List 4, 'Company performance', Question 4.11 and the answers to Questions 4.19 and 4.20 indicate that the proportion is correct/incorrect?

9.77 What steps can be taken to bring about any changes needed?

9.78 How many calls are dedicated to seeking new business? (See List 4, 'Company performance', Questions 4.11 and 4.20.)

9.79 Has any attempt been made to profile prospects with a high business possibility? (See Introduction and List 13, 'The buying process', Questions 13.41 and 13.42.)

9.80 How many first approaches does it take, on average, in order to develop a meaningful dialogue?

9.81 How frequently does top management accompany salesmen on calls?

9.82 How frequently does top management meet customers visiting plant or office?

9.83 To what extent is telephone selling used?

9.84 Could the sales effort be supported by telephone selling?

9.85 What is the procedure for handling direct enquiries/orders?

9.86 Is it formal, understood, and complied with?

9.87 What are the salesmen's views on the internal handling of direct enquiries/orders?

9.88 What are customers' views on the handling of direct enquiries/orders?

9.89 What changes are required to allow for any salesmen's/customers' expressed needs and criticisms?

9.90 Is there any history of mishandled direct enquiries/orders?

9.91 What steps have been taken to prevent re-occurrence? (See Introduction relating to the above seven questions.)

9.92 How is the salesman notified of direct enquiries from his territory? (Compare answer with Question 9.20.)

9.93 Is the salesman notified of deliveries into his territory?

9.94 Is the salesman notified of any change in status of his customers, particularly credit rating? (See List 24, 'Product/service financial information', Question 24.36.)

9.95 Do the salesmen provide a full report on their activities?

9.96 Is it a narrative report or a formal document?

9.97 Does the reporting system yield market information? (See Introduction to List 6, 'Marketing information: systems and use', and Question 6.8.)

9.98 Does the salesmen's reporting system require reasons for lost business to be given? (See List 14, 'Analysing lost business', Question 14.1.)

9.99 Does the reporting system encourage salesmen to give 'price' as a reason?

9.100 Is a 'price' response probed?

Appendix 9A. Model for company report-back system[1]

Sales representative:_____   Region:_____

	September 1981 £	Six-months cumulative £	Best salesman cumulative £

Volume sales
- Institutional
- Commercial
- Total sales
- Budgeted sales

	Monthly sales £	Budget GP %	Cumulative sales £	Actual cumulative GP £	Cumulative sales £	Actual cumulative GP £

Product mix
- Sensitized paper
- Tracing paper
- Drafting Machines
- Printing Machines
- Ancillaries
- Job printing

	On budgeted sales at budgeted percentages	Actual GP	Budgeted GP on budgeted sales	Actual GP

Gross profit

	Budgeted	Actual	Budgeted	Actual

expenses (cumulative)
- Your selling expenses
- 400% regional overheads
- 50% head office overheads
- Total cumulative expenses
  attributable to your sales

1. Adapted from a company report-back format developed by J. B. Madden.

Net profit

	Yours monthly	Yours cumulative	Best salesman's cumulative
Personal statistics			
Total orders booked (no.)			
Total calls made (no.)			
Reports submitted (no.)			
Days worked in the field (days)			
Time spent with customers (hrs)			
New prospects (no.)			
Number of orders cancelled			
Value of orders cancelled			
Advertisements discussed on calls			
Your efficiency index			
Calls per day			
Percentage of orders to calls			
Average value of order			
Personal sacrifice			
Nights spent away from home			
Your cumulative commission			
$1\frac{1}{2}$% sensitized and tracing paper			
2% job printing			
$\frac{1}{2}$% rest			
TOTAL			

Your all-England ranking	1. A. Green	2. F. Brown	3. S. Patel	4. J. Smith
Branch ranking	1. West	2. East	3. South	4. North

Appendix 9B.   Cost per call calculations

	(£)
Recruitment	159
Remuneration	7170
Company vehicle	1735
Expenses	2741
Sales manager (including secretarial expenses and overheads)	868
Area manager (including expenses and overheads)	1975
Wages calculation	47
Sales analysis	232
Secretarial (including overheads)	589
Stationery	505
Training	162
TOTAL	116,183[2]

Calls per day	8
Orders per day	2 (25%)
Working days per annum	220
Total calls per annum	1760
Total orders per annum	440
Sales cost per call: cost ÷ calls	£9.19
Sales cost per order: cost ÷ orders	£36.77

2. *Financial Times* and Sales Force Ltd.

List 10. The agency system

Introduction

Attitudes towards the use of agents tend to polarize between those firms who operate totally with agents, most particularly overseas, and those who prefer not to have any at all. 'Agents', it is argued, 'sell what's selling'; 'They carry so many lines they are not interested in any of them'; 'The agent is in business for himself, not us'—all are frequently heard typical comments.

In fact, agents do have a role to play, and it is wrong to take up rigid attitudes based on history or hearsay without a real consideration of the 'plusses' and 'minuses' of using agents.

The first and overriding point to be considered is that, despite the fact they operate on what is called a 'contingency pay pricing' (payment by results) basis, they cost money to acquire and maintain. Samples, catalogues, brochures, visits, stocks, correspondence, telex, telephone calls, training, etc.—all take time, and all cost the firm something. It is important, therefore, that their performance not only justifies the investment the principal makes in them, but shows a *pro rata* profit commensurate both to that produced by the directly employed sales force and relative to the cost of maintaining the agent.

It is possible, of course, to run an agency system with minimum costs. However, these usually produce a high turnover of agents and a low input of orders. The rule must be that, if agents are to be used, they should be supported in every way and used well. They must be made to feel part of the company, not outsiders. As with directly employed salesmen, motivation is vital, and as with own salesmen, motivation is not simply a question of money.

The major problem with agents is finding them. Good agents, particularly overseas, are few and far between, and generally speaking are not 'hungry' for new lines and new principals. There has to be something about the firm and its offerings to tempt them. There is as much a marketing job to be done in acquiring agents as in disposing of a firm's output. List 5, 'Export marketing', Appendix 5A gives a staged process for obtaining and monitoring agents. It should be studied in conjunction with this list because of the similarity of the problems and tasks involved.

One major international manufacturer of automotive batteries found that his sales organization was disintegrating with an ageing agency force. Replacement from conventional sources was proving impossible. He decided therefore that if agents did not exist he would have to create them, which he proceeded to do with great success by converting many of his directly employed salesmen to agents, assisting them with extended credit, occasionally some capital, and other forms of financial and non-financial support. The system was rebuilt successfully within two years.

The check list can be extended by many of the questions in List 9, 'The sales force', and should certainly be completed in conjunction with List 5, 'Export marketing'.

Too often where a mixed system of direct sales and agents is used, responsibility for agents within the company is diffused and in any event is a marginal activity. Question 10.9 calls for a closer look at this situation, particularly when the high cost (in every respect) of recruitment is considered.

Performance is indeed the outcome of effective agent recruitment, induction, and maintenance. In recruiting, the minimum performance expectation (and the time to achieve it) should always be stated to avoid subsequent failure for both parties. Once operating, the agents should have a clear idea of what is expected of them (and conversely what the principal will do for the agent). Developing performance standards, which Question 10.30 covers, for personnel over whom there is little control other than terminating the agency, requires tact, advocacy and a lively awareness of conditions in the agent's territory and indeed within the agency itself.

Questions 10.45–10.48 cover the thorny problem of getting the agents to report on their activities—something that can be demanded from an employed sales force. The fact that agents often resent what they see as a piece of bureaucracy or an interference in their business is because they do not know how the information is used. If firms demand agents' reports they are at the very least obligated to show how they will be used for the principal's and the agent's benefit.

Question 10.49 requires financial analysis of the cost of maintaining agents and calls for a compilation of all the cost items involved. This list will be longer than the items previously referred to in this introduction and must include the cost of recruitment. Only if this figure is added will it become apparent, first, if an agency system is viable and, second, how important it is to retain agencies and not to allow the system to atrophy.

Question 10.54 is an interesting one. Too many firms treat direct orders from an agent's territory or large orders as 'house accounts'. This may seem justified in financial terms, but the wider picture ought to be scrutinized before a decision of this sort is taken. Sharing a commission with the agent could produce a far more rewarding result than the commission saved. The same rule applies to hybrid orders, that is, where an order is placed in one territory for delivery in another, for example with central group purchasing of builders' supplies going into branches.

The final questions, 10.58–10.62, look at agency agreements. It is always wise to have a written statement of an understanding, most particularly a statement of performance requirements, but the marketing auditor must always ask himself how far his company would go to maintain the terms of an agreement. If the principal would not in reality insist on full compliance, then obviously it must be asked whether the restrictions in the agreement do more than create an irritant rather than a method of control.

It is always well to remember that the agent is a freelance operator who is indeed in business for himself. It is the job of the principal to make sure that the interest of both parties is aligned. This way the agency system can be profitable and relativey trouble-free. The care and feeding of agents is as crucial a marketing function as any other covered in these check lists.

The first questions apply only to firms *not* using agents. Later questions relate to firms either considering their use or already employing them.

10.1 What were the reasons in the past for not using agents?

10.2 Are they still valid?

10.3 What circumstances would have to exist before we would consider appointing agents?

10.4 Is there any territory/industry/application, etc., uncovered or covered inadequately by our sales force?

10.5 Would agents be able to fill the gap?

10.6 What would the agents have to provide in the way of facilities/coverage/services, etc., before the question of adopting an agency system would be considered? (Use the services categorization in List 3, 'The service element in marketing', Appendix 3A, as an *aide memoire* as to the agencies' expected role as part of the selling organization.)

10.7 What technical experience or qualifications for agents are required?

10.8 Is the requirement rigid?

10.9 If we had/have agents, who in the company was, is, or would be responsible for them?

10.10 What proportion of that person's time was, is, or will be devoted to managing the agency structure?

10.11 How was, is, or will the responsibility be discharged and reported?

10.12 What other products/manufacturers represented would be regarded as compatible/incompatible with our requirements? (See also answer to Question 10.53 and List 17, 'Competitive climate', Questions 17.42 and 17.44.)

10.13 Are there any firms we would not be willing to share an agent with? (See also answer to Question 10.53.)

10.14 What is the function of the agency system (e.g., all sales, support function for own sales force, expediency, special circumstances)?

10.15 Are they aware of the role they play in our sales organization?

10.16 Do they fulfil the function we have designated to them?

10.17 If not, how can it be re-orientated?

10.18 What is the target number of agencies and their geographical locations?

10.19 What has stopped us filling any vacancies? Identify constraints.

10.20 Are the constraints immutable, or can we adjust policy to resolve the problem?

10.21 Have we a screening system for agency recruitment? (See also List 5, 'Export marketing', Appendix 5A, Stage 5.)

10.22 What is the history of agent acquisition and loss?

10.23 Does it show a common pattern of losses?

10.24 Is this pattern a reflection of recruitment, induction, support methods or business conditions?

10.25 What techniques do we use to recruit agents (advertising, asking customers, professional or trade associations, etc.)? (See List 5, 'Export marketing', Appendix 5A, Stage 7.)

10.26 Which are the most effective?

10.27 Are our agencies exclusive?

10.28 Would agency retention and performance improve with any change from/to exclusive arrangements?

10.29 Is agency performance monitored?

10.30 What are the performance standards?

10.31 How were they arrived at?

10.32 Do the agents understand and accept them?

10.33 What happens with constant under-performance?

10.34 Are agents visited regularly by senior management in the company?

10.35 What is the purpose of such visits?

10.36 Do agents approve or dislike them?

10.37 When was the last time each agent visited us?

10.38 What is the purpose of such visits?

10.39 Are the number of visits to us regarded as satisfactory by us and by the agents?

10.40 What support (sales aids, stocks, credit, joint advertising, order referral, etc.) do our agents expect? (To expand on these prompts see List 11, 'Non-personal promotion: methods and media', Question 11.1.)

10.41 What facilities do our agents provide? (Compare answer with Question 10.6.)

10.42 How far do we meet their expectations and do they meet ours in regard to support?

10.43 What actions can and should be taken to bring expectations more into line?

10.44 What constraints prevent us from taking these actions?

10.45 Are agents expected to report on their activities (sales calls, enquiries, quotations, advertising, etc.)?

10.46 Are these reports regarded as onerous?

10.47 How do we utilize this information?

10.48 Can the agents see any evidence of the use of their reports? (See Introduction, and also questions relating to the information role of the salesman in List 9, 'The sales force', Questions 9.95–9.98.)

10.49 What are the elements of cost of agency support (samples, stocks, visits, entertainment, training, communication, etc.)? (See Introduction.)

10.50 How much does each agency cost us to support? (See Introduction.)

10.51 How profitable is each agency?

10.52 Assess the degree of interest the agent has in our products. (See also answer to Question 10.12.)

10.53 Who are his most important principals? (See answer to Question 10.13 and also List 17, 'Competitive climate', Questions 17.43 and 17.44.)

10.54 How are orders received directly from the agents' territory treated in regard to agents' commission?

10.55 If direct orders are 'house accounts', assess the cost of giving the agent part or whole commission against the likelihood of increased loyalty and interest engendered, or alternatively loss of agency interest and thus lost sales opportunities.

10.56 How vulnerable are our agents to our competitors' reaching an agreement with them? (See also List 17, 'Competitive climate', Question 17.42.)

10.57 What steps can we take to protect ourselves?

10.58 Do we have formal contracts with agents?

10.59 Are they comprehensive?

10.60 Do we or our agents regard them as over-restrictive?

10.61 Can agreement compliance be checked?

10.62 What actions would we take in an agreement breach?

List 11. Non-personal promotion: methods and media

Introduction

The marketing communication process, of which of course the salesman is a vital part, is perhaps appropriately expressed at this stage. At its simplest, the task of marketing is to move the prospective purchaser from a condition of ignorance about the firm and its products/services, reputation, and customers, to a state of knowledge, then to achieve an understanding of the message that the marketer is conveying, leading to a belief in its accuracy. Only when these stages have been accomplished will buying action take place. It has never been better illustrated than in the model shown in Fig. 11-1 on page 108.[1]

A benchmark check on the level of awareness/unawareness can give an absolute answer which is of considerable value in measuring progress. As has already been stated in the Introduction to List 4, 'Company performance', it is an 'absolute' in marketing that if you are not known people cannot buy from you.

Measuring or evaluating the extent to which the message is understood is more difficult and essentially qualitative, as indeed is the study of 'conviction'. Nevertheless, for all the problems of evaluation of non-personal selling methods the attempt should be made on an on-going basis. Questions 11.19–11.21 examine these points.

But to return to the early questions. Question 11.1 lists some of the many tools and techniques available to the marketer; despite its length, it is not complete. Every auditor will be able to add other items if he so chooses. Because of the length of the compilation it cuts across many questions in this and other lists. Not all of these are cross-referenced, since many of them will be obvious.

To achieve purchasing action the choice of marketing tools and media is bewilderingly wide, as can be seen, and, for industrial goods and services at least, largely unconsidered. Some valuable techniques are ignored in all types of marketing activity, however, because marketers consider many tools inappropriate for reasons ranging from cost to image. While there may be some validity in reasons for rejection, all too rarely do firms reconsider the basis of their original objection and whether the conditions on which it was based have not changed so as to permit the adoption of the promotional methods not attempted previously.

Another major reason for neglect is of course ignorance. Some of the promotional methods listed are unknown or improperly understood by marketers, most particularly by marketers of industrial goods and services and of professional services. For example, many

---

1. A. H. Colley, 'Squeezing the waste out of advertising', *Harvard Business Review*, Cambridge Mass., September/October, 1962.

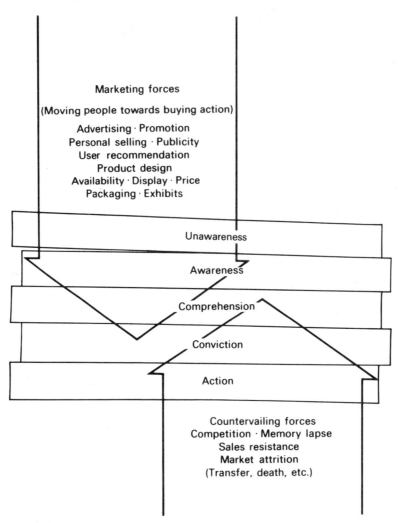

Figure 11-1 Marketing communication process

of them are unaware of the sponsored book, which is a magnificent, frequently self-liquidating method of promotion. Competitions are seen as strictly corn flake marketing, whereas they have been used with great success by both prestigious professional service companies and mundane office supplies firms.

Thus the marketing auditor must resist the temptation to ignore any tools or methods that are not known or understood from their title. He should seek more information, which is easily obtainable from any of a large range of excellent books on marketing. Only with a knowledge of any particular technique is it possible to decide on its cost effectiveness within the current or planned activities of the firm. Questions 11.3–11.9 call for the reconsideration of either criteria or state of knowledge.

In List 4, 'Company performance', it was suggested that the only accurate way of finding out which promotion (and, indeed, which salesmen and agents) are effective is to trace the source of enquiries and the conversion rate to business. Question 11.10 now puts a new element in the 'mix' in that a comparison is called for of expenditure between media, industry, applications, and other factors to see if there is a relationship between these and business obtained.[2] In other words, is time and talent perhaps being expended in, say, a specific industry campaign while business in fact emanates from another industry or from another promotion technique? If the promotional results are taken in a blanket form a number of incorrect—dangerously and expensively incorrect—assumptions may be made. Just as much as marketing strategy calls for segmentation, so does promotion. Question 1.20 in List 1, 'Marketing strategy and planning', anticipated the point that has now been reached. An alignment between market segmentations and promotional activity is vital for success and economy.

Taking the analysis to its logical conclusion, answering Question 11.17 will display the strengths and weaknesses of all marketing activity. It will also reveal the quality of sales calls and provide information on the audience for different methods of non-personal promotion. Given that an objective is to obtain sales, raising a high number of unconverted enquiries would indicate a medium or method weakness. This is not, of course, to ignore any 'visibility' improvement and its long-term implications. In a sense this is the same situation as the low selling product's marketing (as opposed to revenue) contribution, referred to in the List 2, 'Product/service range', Introduction.

The suggestion that the most practical way of assessing marketing effectiveness is to attempt to relate enquiries and ultimately orders to any given marketing activity is nevertheless a very simplistic approach in that the various marketing methods interface, sometimes inextricably; not all customers can recall with accuracy their original sources of information, and competitors' marketing activities can impact **on the** firm's marketing result. It may be crude but some form of evaluation is not only desirable, but necessary.

Question 11.17 is perhaps the most difficult, but also one of the most critical, in the entire check lists. Without some guidelines as to what in the marketing mix is working, there is no point in attempting to guide and control the marketing methods.

Question 11.39 identifies what for many firms can be a source of considerable wastage. The auditor is strongly recommended to study a number of excellent check lists specific to evaluating exhibitions, in terms of whether to exhibit, post-exhibition results analysis, and visiting exhibitions.[3]

Question 11.40 should not be attempted until the auditor is clear as to just what the promotional expenditure was intended to achieve. If it was 'visibility', then there is no justification to say it failed if sales were not immediately increased. Effectiveness is essentially the test of what has occurred since the promotion took place as compared with the objectives.

Question 11.41 calls for salesmen's views of the advertising and other promotional expenditure. Salesmen do tend to regard all non-personal selling promotion as substantially wasteful and frequently irrelevant. Nothing could be further from the truth. Media advertising, to take just one tool, is complementary to personal selling but with a different function. If the sales force cannot see how this assists them in their task, then management has failed miserably in its communications and with training of their salesmen. It is worth pausing to consider that differences between selling and advertising are not just semantic (see table overleaf).

---

2. The ratios will have been provided by the auditor's answers to List 4, 'Company performance', Questions 4.24 and 4.25, and this same analysis relative to one marketing tool—personal selling—will have been given in List 9, 'The sales force', Questions 9.47–9.49.

3. Alfred Alles, *Exhibitions: Universal Marketing Tools*, Associated Business Programmes, London, 1973.

Features of selling	Features of advertising	
	Operational	*General*
• Flexibility: the message can be tailored precisely to the prospect's needs	• Impersonal	• Creates awareness
	• Easily accessible	• Gives knowledge
	• General interest only	• Produces some level of attitude change or formation
• Comprehensiveness: the most complex sales messages can be communicated and explained	• One-way communication	
	• Persuasive	
• Attention-getting: personal selling obtains and maintains a high level of attention		

The same problem does not arise with intermediaries who like to see a heavy volume of advertising addressed to their customers (rather than to themselves), because they appreciate the role a promotion can play in making it easier for them to sell. If this acceptance can be achieved among intermediaries, it must be asked why sales forces have been so slow to view non-personal selling as a sales aid. This is an area in which marketing management can achieve a great deal to obtain better mileage from promotional expenditure. It has been said with considerable truth that marketing's greatest failure is its inability to sell marketing to the sales force. Here is an area where synergy can be introduced to everyone's benefit.

Many businessmen have become somewhat cynical about directories since they have been the subject of the most persistent of confidence tricks over the years. Any businessman who falls into this trap, which is so easy to avoid, deserves sympathy and nothing else. However, in the attempt to avoid fake directories many valuable genuine ones can be omitted. Question 11.47 calls for a full review periodically of all relevant directories, year books and buyers' guides, and the decision on entry should be taken for each new edition not automatically. A study of 500 businesses' sources of information for products and services revealed the classified directories as the single most important medium. It is not often realized that, while the alphabetical telephone directories cover only the relevant geographical areas, firms can take entries in the yellow pages in any part of the country. It is cheap and effective, and all research shows it is heavily used.

Finally, Question 11.53, brief as it is, has valuable implications for most companies and usually reveals opportunities unexploited. Most guarantees are historical rather than realistic, and a simple analysis of the cost of fulfilling guarantee claims such as will be sought in List 24, 'Product/service financial information'. The answer to Question 24.41 will very clearly show how far a guarantee can be extended without the situation leading to losses. A manufacturer of garment finishing equipment gave the conventional 12-month guarantee on his equipment. Guarantee claims in the first 36 months were negligible and would in any event have been met without a guarantee. He was thus able to offer a five-year guarantee at a budget cost which previously applied to 12 months and consequently had a very considerable 'plus' to promote. A long and unequivocal guarantee is a public affirmation of faith in the product, and as such it is a valuable marketing tool usually grossly neglected.

The whole of this check list should be viewed against what the objectives, the various methods, media, and expenditures of time and money are expected to achieve. Within an organization it is commonplace for a wide range of views to exist as to what a marketing campaign or a marketing tool is supposed to accomplish. A media advertising campaign may well be seen by the chairman as having as its purpose image improvement; the sales manager expects it to help in reducing inventory; the works manager seeks a better spread of demand over machine and labour capacity; the personnel director hopes it will attract the best graduates to the firm. If it succeeds in only one of these it will be said to have failed in the others. If this type of disappointment and resultant criticism is to be avoided, objectives must always be specific and practical and clearly understood by all who are involved.

11.1 Which of the following promotional methods have been/are being used, or have been considered and rejected?

	Used now	Used in the past	Considered and rejected	Not considered
Telephone selling				
Media advertising (including radio and TV)				
Public/press relations				
Merchandising techniques				
Pricing strategies				
Range strategies				
Interpersonal network				
Backing services				
Marketing research				
Competitions and interactive marketing				
Company visits				
Directories/year books				
Incentive schemes				
Design				
Product/packaging				
Exhibitions				
Gifts				
Franchise dealings				
Financial incentives and aids				
Reciprocal trading				
Guarantee manipulation				
Direct mail				

	Used now	Used in the past	Considered and rejected	Not considered
Distribution				
Demonstrations and reference plant				
Sampling				
Lotteries				
Secondments				
Posters				
Client training				
Couponing				
Educational campaigns				
Loan equipment				
Co-operative promotions				
Full-range buying schemes				
Viewdata				
Premium offers				
Trade-in allowances				
Re-use container premiums				
Lead time				
Sponsorships (events, books, academic)				
Vehicle livery				
Brochures and catalogues (including catalogue distribution and information services)				
Audio-visual				
Off-premises displays				
Loyalty schemes				

11.2 Give current appropriation (state period) for each tool used.

11.3 What method was used for arriving at the non-personal marketing appropriation?

11.4 Are the targets and objectives qualitative and quantitative for each of the methods used, clearly set out, and known within the company? (See List 21, 'Images and perceptions', Question 21.32.)

11.5 Relate the decision-making unit (DMU) target to each method used and justify in terms of effectiveness and numbers. (See List 13, 'The buying process', Questions 13.7 and 13.8.)

11.6 Are the reasons for discontinuing any previously used tools still valid?

11.7 What criteria were used in deciding to reject any particular marketing method not previously tried?

11.8 Are the criteria still valid?

11.9 What knowledge do we have of methods not used and not considered? (See Introduction.)

11.10 What is the marketing expenditure broken down by?

	Year	Amount
Method		
Medium		
Season		
Geographical area		
Industry		
Application		
Product/service		

(Relate answers to those given in List 1, 'Marketing strategy and planning', Question 1.20, concerning segment priorities and Introduction to List 4, 'Company performance').

11.11 How does this compare with previous years?

11.12 What is the reason for any variation?

11.13 How does the expenditure compare with sources of business obtained using the same breakdowns?

11.14 Does it show an imbalance?

11.15 Could this be rectified by an adjustment in the appropriation or the appropriation allocation?

11.16 What is the cost of marketing (other than personal selling)?

- Per enquiry
- Per quotation
- Per order
- By media
- By method

(This information will also be required to answer List 24, 'Product/service financial information', Question 24.40.)

11.17 Relate value of enquiries/orders received to any traceable medium or method. (Cross-relate answer to Questions 11.1 and 11.2.)

11.18 What methods of evaluation of effectiveness of total marketing and of individual tools are used? (This information is referred to again in List 24, 'Product/service financial information', Question 24.40.)

11.19 Do we know the past and current level of 'visibility'? (See Introduction and Question 11.49 and also Introduction to List 4, 'Company performance'.)

11.20 Can we evaluate to what extent the messages we convey are understood?

11.21 Can we evaluate the market's level of conviction that our message carries?

11.22 How often is an evaluation of effectiveness made?

11.23 How does the firm's marketing history and performance compare with competitors? (See List 17, 'Competitive climate', Question 17.45.)

11.24 Are any differences justified by comparative performances?

11.25 What are the principle media used?

11.26 What is the justification for these?

11.27 Are the facts on which the justification was based still valid (changes in product/services, markets, economy, publication circulation in numbers, audience and quality of readership, growth of competitive media, e.g., radio, TV, Viewdata)?

11.28 What is the copy strategy used for the firm's products/services during the last five years (i.e., to obtain visibility, unaided recall, image development, sell products/services, etc.)? (See Introduction and Fig. 11-1.)

11.29 What are the major changes and causes of change in copy strategy that have occurred in the last five years? (Compare answer with List 21, 'Images and perceptions', Question 21.32.)

11.30 To what type of advertising and media are users and potential users most exposed? (See List 16, 'User industries', Question 16.56.)

11.31 How does this analysis compare to our media schedule?

11.32 When was advertising policy, expenditure, schedules and strategy last reviewed?

11.33 Does advertising and other promotional material emphasize benefits, features, and any unique selling propositions or other differentiated advantages? (See Introduction to List 2, 'Product/service range', Questions 2.27 and 2.28, and List 4, 'Company performance', Question 4.2.)

11.34 Does our promotion identify any unique selling proposition or differentiated advantage? (See Introduction to List 2, 'Product/service range', and Question 2.42.)

11.35 Do competitors handle their own advertising or use agencies?

11.36 How does this differ from our policy and how is it justified?

11.37 What is the audience (in numbers) for each specific method of promotion?

11.38 Which exhibitions have we and our competitors shown at in the last year(s)? (See Introduction concerning more detailed exhibition check lists.)

11.39 Have we any analysis of total attendance, stand visits, enquiries received, business booked?

11.40 Should we review continued showing at all/any exhibition(s)?

11.41 What is the sales force view on the effectiveness of advertising and other promotion methods? (See Introduction.)

11.42 Would they make any changes, and if so in what way?

11.43 What are intermediaries' views on advertising and other promotional effectiveness? (See Introduction.)

11.44 Which of the methods listed and used in Question 11.1 have been undertaken by ourselves, agencies, consultants, or other specialists? (Cross-reference the answer to this question and Question 11.35 and to List 21, 'Images and perceptions', Question 21.34.)

11.45 How successful were our efforts as compared with outside contractors?

11.46 Does the result of this analysis call for a review of policy in relation to the use of external contractors?

11.47 Which directories, year books and buyers guides do we appear in? Is the list complete/efficient? What are their 'shelf' lives?

11.48 Is our policy on the use of brands valid?

11.49 Does our brand as compared with the firm have 'visibility' and a good image? (See answer to Question 11.19 and List 21, 'Images and perceptions', Question 21.14.)

11.50 Would we benefit by increasing/decreasing brand promotion?

11.51 How long and how comprehensive are our guarantees? (See Introduction and also the answer to List 22, 'Non-differentiated products', Questions 22.20 and 22.24, and the analysis called for in List 24, 'Product/service financial information', Question 24.41.)

11.52 How do our guarantees compare with those of our competitors and general trade practice? (See List 17, 'Competitive climate', Question 17.46.)

11.53 What would it cost us to extend our guarantees in coverage and in time by, say, 3 months? 6 months? 9 months? 1 year? (See List 22, 'Non-differentiated products', Question 22.21, and List 24, 'Product/service financial information', Question 24.41.)

List 12.   The distributive system

Introduction

The term 'distributor' is used generically in the check list that follows to include all types of intermediaries who buy and sell in their own right as opposed to agents operating on a commission basis. Thus the nomenclatures 'stockist', 'wholesaler', 'dealer', 'merchant', 'importer', 'broker', etc., are all embraced by the term 'distributor'.

The decision to trade direct or through re-sellers is a very basic one, and the correct decision must influence the performance of the company favourably. Mixed systems do work, although there is plenty of evidence of an antipathy by distributors towards manufacturers who compete directly with them, and naturally there is a reluctance to support such suppliers. Questions 12.1 and 12.2 are concerned with this basic decision.

The problem of distributors, as with agents, has been summed up as being that 'they carry so many lines they are not interested in any of them'. While, like most exaggerations, it contains some truth, a rectification of such a situation is not beyond the skills of any manufacturer who understands the interests and problems of distributors. It is up to suppliers to obtain and retain distributor loyalty and interest, and this is not only a question of margins.

Marketing auditors may find that many of the questions in List 5, 'Export marketing', relating to representation, can also be used in the profiling of distributors, their selection and monitoring, in so far as there is any choice in the use of distributors and the decision is not pre-empted by lack of choice.

In a changing world the role of the distributor in most trades is also changing. Indeed, there is some evidence to suggest that, increasingly, manufacturers prefer to keep the communication channels with the end-customer short. But where distributors are used there is an international trend, as already noted, for the most efficient suppliers to tie up in some form or another the most efficient distributors, leaving the less successful suppliers with the second-line distributors—a toxic combination. All suppliers need to look with increasing frequency at the distributive methods they use and be ready and able to make changes when the moment occurs. Indeed, distributors, or lack of them, may be a major vulnerability of many suppliers.

It is not of course necessary to view the distributive system as a single-level structure. It is perfectly possible, and indeed often sensible, to develop a tiered system of, for example, preferential distributors. Firms selected on a preferential basis receive additional support in a number of ways and give an incentive to non-preferential distributors to develop their own operations to reach preferential status. A multi-tiered system has long been used in the automotive industry. Questions 12.7 and 12.8 raise this issue.

Another form of preferential or exclusive trading is of course through franchise, licence or solus operations which are all well worth considering. Franchising and solus trading are now very big business indeed, but for a franchise or solus deal to operate successfully, the supplier must have something very specific to offer if the franchise or solus trader is to accept the constraints imposed by each system. To obtain some idea of the mutual commitments of franchisor and franchisee, it is only necessary to look at some of the successful consumer goods and service operations. The subject is too vast, and its ramifications too complex, to be encompassed in this check list, but market auditors are recommended to investigate the advantages of the systems if they themselves meet the criteria for franchisor and the prospective franchisees or solus traders exist or can be created. Question 12.17 seeks an examination of the gains and losses of a franchise or other form of exclusive trading system.[1]

Needless to say, distributors' major interest will be the margins they can achieve, but they are not insensitive to the costs they will be involved in handling, installing, servicing, or exchanging products. Ideally, the distributor would like a non-return valve in the distributive pipe-line, so that when a product is sold all further responsibility ends. This of course cannot be so, but clearly the distributors' loyalty and interest will be with the suppliers whose products cause the least aggravation, whatever the source of it may be.

There is a dichotomy in distributors' thinking on price. While a high price with usually the same percentage margin means a higher return on the product, it does become more difficult to sell. A lower price with higher aggregate sales may give a better result in total. Either possibility can be promoted effectively, but suppliers' practice is often to impose a price without discussion or consideration of the distributors' needs and requirements.

Just as agencies cost the firm money to maintain, so do distributors. The questions posed in Questions 12.54–12.56 seek to identify when it is more profitable not to sell through distributors than to incorporate them in the marketing system. At the same time, it is always important not to allow a high sales potential distributor to be dropped because of perhaps current depressed sales. It is wrong to adopt a mechanistic approach, and every under-performing distributor needs to be looked at as an individual case before any decision is taken.

Sales aids, referred to in Question 12.65, can be as important to the distributor as they are to the salesmen, but frequently this is not appreciated. As with salesmen, distributors have to be taught and persuaded to use aids, often expensively produced. The bulk of sales aids, most particularly point-of-sale display items, either are not used, are used incorrectly, or are used and discarded too quickly, long before the end of their useful life. There should be a constant check of sales aid requirements and use.

Finally, there is a generally held view that services cannot be distributed since they cannot be stocked. This is a piece of pure academic nonsense designed to fit the conventional theory that services are always totally intangible, that they are consumed at the moment of production, and that the buyer of services must take part in their production. (See List 23, 'Service businesses').[2] Services can indeed be distributed. Nothing could better illustrate this than the distributive system for financial services (Fig. 12-1). Other services that lean heavily on a distributive system are contract cleaning, pest control, copy shops, laundrettes, and security.

1. Two useful guides to franchising are M. Mendelsohn and D. Acheson, *How to Franchise your Business*, and M. Mendelsohn, *How to Evaluate a Franchise*, Franchise Publications, London, 1980.
2. Edwin Ornstein, *The Marketing of Money*, Gower Press, Farnborough, 1972.

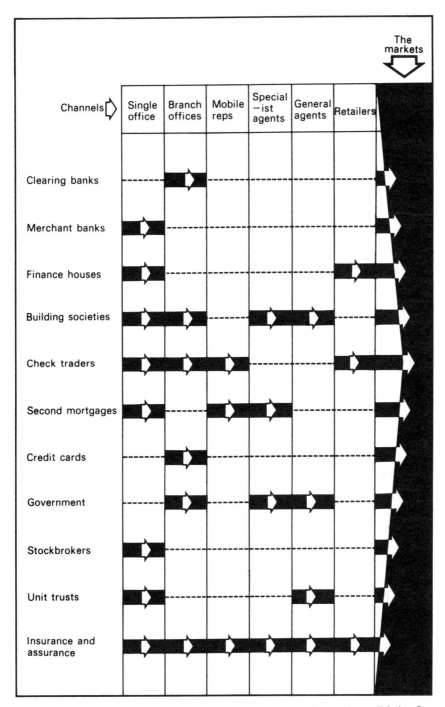

Figure 12-1 Alternative channels of distribution of money products (from Edwin Ornstein, *The Marketing of Money*, Gower, Farnborough 1972)

12.1 What criteria are/were applied to decide whether distributors shall be used?

12.2 Are the criteria still valid?

12.3 If distributors are used, how many, when, where, and what volume of business is transacted through them? (This question was asked previously in List 4, 'Company performance', Question 4.27.)

12.4 What types of distributors are used?

12.5 Are intermediaries selected, or are our sales efforts directed to all available outlets?

12.6 If selectivity is applied, what are the criteria for selection of intermediaries?

12.7 Have we considered a multi-tiered system of preferential distributors? (See Introduction.)

12.8 What is the basis for selection or preferential treatment, e.g., turnover, stock levels held, quality of service, etc.? (See Introduction.)

12.9 What evidence is there that conditions are met?

12.10 What happens if they are not met?

12.11 Could we significantly increase our distribution coverage by changes in appointment conditions or the development of a multi-tiered system?

12.12 What is the policy on increasing/decreasing the use of distributors at home/overseas? (Compare answer to Question 12.69.)

12.13 What are/were the reasons for the policy?

12.14 Approximately how many distributors of the product are there in the market as a whole?

12.15 What percentage of these do we supply?

12.16 What limits additional coverage?

12.17 Would there be benefits in operating a franchise or solus arrangement? (See Introduction.)

12.18 If so, what would they **be**? Are they sufficient to warrant setting up franchise or solus distributors?

12.19 What benefits would we be able to offer a franchisor?

- Know-how
- Promotion of product/service
- Local promotion of franchise
- Financial assistance
- Administrative procedures
- Financial controls
- Preferential purchasing deals

- Training
- Support stocks
- Credit
- Recruitment aid
- Geographical exclusivity
- Identification with franchise subject

12.20 What do we expect from a franchisor?

- No competitive trading
- Agreed stock holding level
- Right to purchase back franchise
- Clear identification with us
- Information on performance
- Staffing—quality and numbers
- Purchase of supplies from designated source

- Minimum performance standards (sales)
- Maintenance of premises and/or equipment to agreed standards
- Financial commitments
- Display and merchandising
- Consistent quality of service at agreed levels
- Selling prices as set

12.21 Would sales prospects be improved by adopting/dropping/liberalizing a selectivity policy?

12.22 What other types of products/services do our distributors sell: directly competitive, indirectly competitive, non-competitive?

12.23 How do products/services of our type rate in terms of importance and interest to distributors?

12.24 Within this group, how do our firm's products/services rate in terms of importance and interest to the distributor?

12.25 What would make them more interesting to distributors?

12.26 What policies could we adopt that would increase distributor interest and activity in and with our products/services?

12.27 What are our distributor sales by type of distributor, size of distributor, geographical location, industrial concentration, etc. (See List 4, 'Company performance', Question 4.27.)

12.28 How does this compare with our competitors? (List 17, 'Competitive climate', Question 17.36, will require use of this same answer.)

12.29 Is any difference advantageous/disadvantageous to us?

12.30 Which competitors make the most and least use of distributors for the products under review?

12.31 How do we account for their policies?

12.32 How and why does it differ from our policy?

12.33 (If also selling direct:) Do salesmen participate in distributor sales and do they service distributors?

12.34 Are salesmen rewarded for distributor business whether obtained by them or received direct?

12.35 If not, would distributor sales and service be improved by changing salesmen remuneration to incorporate distributor sales?

12.36 How are direct sales in distributors' territory handled? (Compared with List 9, 'The sales force', Question 9.20.)

12.37 Would a change of policy on direct sales improve/decrease distributor sales and interest? (Compare answers with Questions 12.25–12.26.)

12.38 What stocks are normally held by distributors? (See answer in List 17, 'Competitive climate', Question 17.12.)

12.39 Are there seasonal variations?

12.40 What factors would induce distributors to even out stock holding?

12.41 What replenishment lead time is required by distributors? (Compare with the answer to List 4, 'Company performance', Question 4.23.)

12.42 How does this compare with direct account requirements?

12.43 Have we considered a rack jobbing tactic, and would it be acceptable to distributors?

12.44 What is the history of out-of-stock situations?

12.45 How far are 'out-of-stocks' our fault and how far the distributors fault? (See answer to List 4, 'Company performance', Question 4.23.)

12.46 What is the size of discounts offered to distributors by the company and competitors? (See List 17, 'Competitive climate', Questions 17.65 and 17.66 and also in relation to the next three questions.)

12.47 What other financial and non-financial incentives do we and our competitors provide?

12.48 How do credit terms compare with competitors?

12.49 How stringent are we on punctuality in payment? (See also List 17, 'Competitive climate', Introduction and answer to Question 17.65.)

12.50 What types of customer/industry do distributors supply (e.g., across all industries, only to small customers)? (The answer to this question should align with List 16, 'User industries', Question 16.17.)

12.51 Are we satisfied with their customer spread?

12.52 Do distributors influence make/brand bought by customers?

12.53 Do they compete for customers with us? If so, to what degree? (See Questions 12.33–12.36.)

12.54 At what level of sales does a distribuive outlet show us a profit?

12.55 Do we take this check at regular intervals?

12.56 If a distributive outlet is not profitable, is it relinquished?

12.57 What allowance is made for a distribution potential in deciding to relinquish a distributor?

12.58 What services do we offer to distributors? (See List 3, 'The service element in marketing', Appendix 3A for list of services.)

12.59 What services do they not get but would like?

12.60 What constraints prevent us from providing them?

12.61 What would the benefits be in terms of increased sales and distributor interest and loyalty from the provision of services?

12.62 What services do distributors provide for their customers? (See List 3, 'The service element in marketing', Appendix 3A, for list of services.)

12.63 Would their sales increase if this improved their services?

12.64 Are there any steps we can take to assist distributors to increase/improve services to their customers?

12.65 What sales and other aids do we provide for distributors? (See Introduction and also compare answer with List 17, 'Competitive climate', Question 17.37.)

12.66 Are they used?

12.67 What evidence is information on their use based (e.g., observation, questioning, requests from distributors, etc.)?

12.68 How often are distributors visited and by whom?

12.69 Is the role of the distributor increasing, decreasing, or remaining constant in importance in the market under review? Why? (Compare with answer to Question 12.12.)

12.70 On what information is the reply based?

12.71 What changes forecast imply a requirement for a change in our policy?

12.72 What is our attitude and policy on 'own brand' trading? (See also List 4, 'Company performance', Questions 4.42 and 4.43.)

List 13. The buying process

Introduction

The end purpose of all marketing is buying, although it would not be thought so judging by the way most marketing books and articles concentrate only on what the marketer should be doing instead of aligning their activities with buying actions in their various sequences and classifications. Literature on the interface between buying and selling is still relatively rare.

This part of the audit intermeshes with every other part, and if there is one list that defies use in isolation, it is this one. The link with selling and non-personal promotion is obvious, as will be the link with lost order analysis and pricing to follow. Only the most important cross-references are given below. This section should be used with all other sections of the marketing audit.

Marketers not familiar with the work of the Marketing Science Institute in the USA into industrial purchasing may find some of the terms used strange.[1] Briefly, the Marketing Science Institute publications recognize four aspects of significance in industrial purchasing: (1) *who buys*—the decision-making unit (DMU); (2) *how do they buy* (a)—the buy phase—an eight-part progression from the recognition of a need to performance (of the supplier firm) feedback; (3) *how do they buy* (b)—the buy class—the classification of purchases into straight re-buys, modified re-buys, and new buys that have important strategic implications; (4) *why do they buy*—the decision-forming factors.

Salesmen tend to call on the person designated as 'buyer', although many others may be involved in a decision to purchase, particularly for a first-time order for a product/service or from a firm. One study of buying practices showed that nearly 80 per cent of board members who were important in purchasing did not see salesmen. The early questions probe the communication targets and, where the DMU is not seen by the salesmen, call for a consideration of the tools that can penetrate to them. In particular, Questions 13.5 and 13.7 should be related to the answers given in List 11, 'Non-personal promotion: methods and media', since it is substantially non-personal techniques that can go behind the buyer without destroying his relationship with the salesman.

The buy class needs at least a crude explanation. Where a firm is an 'outside' contender, because a straight re-buy and even a modified re-buy so strongly favours the 'in' supplier, the only strategy is to attempt to force a consideration of alternatives of which the firm's offering is one. To do this there has to be some innovation, not necessarily technical or patentable, but perhaps in service, guarantees, commercial terms, delivery, etc. Questions 13.11 and 13.13 deal with this position, while 13.4 refers to the opposite strategy, which for the 'in'

---

1. To assist any auditor unfamiliar with the buying/selling interface terms and methods, a short bibliography is given at the end of this list in Appendix 13A.

supplier is to do all possible to hold the purchase as a straight re-buy. The buy class can also have a pervasive effect on the composition of the DMU, which can change in accordance with the purchasing task.

Decision-forming factors will vary depending upon the responsibilities of each member of the DMU. The production manager may be concerned with quality of output, the works manager with the physical dimensions of the equipment, the buyer with price and delivery. The message must be tailored for each person and must also be dynamic, in that an individual member of the DMU's interests, and responsibilities may change as the buying processes proceed. Question 13.17, although short, directs the auditor to a vast and crucial subject.

Question 13.22 is an interesting one. It is not unusual for buying authority to be limited by corporate policy. It may be advisable to adjust the offering so as to put the decision within the authority of a DMU which favours the supplying firm. This can as easily mean, for example, going up in price as going down.

Questions 13.26–13.32, on 'short lists', 'approved suppliers', 'preferred suppliers', are frequently overlooked. The initial marketing task may well be to obtain entry to these lists rather than to sell products. But entry on such lists can also inhibit business. It is commonplace in the automotive industry for a component supplier to be confined to a single component and not be considered for other products. Thus manufacturers of springs are only invited to tender for spring orders and do not have the opportunity of making other offerings. While it is certainly better to be on an approved list for one item than not on at all, firms should be aware of the likelihood of such a list barring approval for a wider range of products or services.

Question 13.35 is, in a sense, a warning that buyers tend to indicate a preference for selling methods that will be found on investigation not to reflect the real situation. Many buyers ask that salesmen do not call and state they prefer to use catalogues. Yet as several studies have shown, over 80 per cent of all industrial sales are closed by salesmen.

The matrices that follow the check list as Appendix 13B bring three of the four aspects of buying together. The first matrix is a model given as an example. Across the top are the individuals and departments that comprise the DMU; down the left-hand side are the eight stages of the buying process; and across the bottom, the factors that are considered by the DMU. The figures represent the factor considered by that member of the DMU at that stage of the buying process. The second matrix is blank. It can be used for deciding the approach to a specific firm or in a specific situation, or it can be adopted for a generalized approach to a particular customer industry. The marketing auditor may find it helpful in completing the matrix to take as an example a recent purchase and trace the DMU, the stages of their involvement and the decision-forming factors.

13.1 Which job functions comprise a typical decision-making unit (DMU) in our customer industries? (See List 16, 'User industries', Question 16.13.)

13.2 Which members of the DMU are outside the company (e.g., architects, consultants, accountants, advertising agencies, distributors, etc.)? (See List 2, 'Product/service range', Introduction and answer to Question 2.19, and List 16, 'User industries', Question 16.47.)

13.3 How does the DMU vary between different purchases (e.g., size, frequency, cost, buy class, lead time, etc.)?

13.4 Which member(s) of the decision-making unit do our salesmen typically see?

13.5 Do we have contact with the other members of the decision-making unit? (See List 11, 'Non-personal promotion: methods and media', Question 11.5.)

13.6 How is this achieved?

13.7 Do our methods create any antagonism with the buyer or buying department? (The answers should be compared with those given in List 11, 'Non-personal promotion: methods and media', Question 11.5, and List 14, 'Analysing lost business', Question 14.6.)

13.8 What overt methods for contacting other members of the DMU can we use without creating antagonisms?

13.9 At what point in the buying continuum is each member of the DMU involved? (See Introduction and Appendix 13B(i), List 14, 'Analysing lost business', Question 14.7, and List 16, 'User industries', Question 16.13.)

13.10 Which factors do each member of the DMU consider at each point of involvement in the purchasing process? (See compilation of some suggested factors in List 16, 'User industries', Questions 16.14 and 16.15.)

13.11 Does the sales approach distinguish between new buy, modified re-buy and straight re-buy situations? (See Introduction.)

13.12 How is information on the buy class gathered and used?

13.13 In the case of a potential customer in a straight re-buy situation, how can we adjust our offering to force a reconsideration of alternatives of which ours will be one? List options. (Some options for forcing a reconsideration are set out in List 22, 'Non-differentiated products'.)

13.14 Where we are the supplying firm, what strategies do we adopt to hold the purchase as a straight re-buy? List options.

13.15 How does the DMU vary in each stage of the buying process? (See Introduction, relative to this and the next three questions.)

13.16 How do the stages of DMU involvement vary in each buy class?

13.17 What are the decision-forming factors in each buy class? (See Introduction to List 2, 'Product/service range', and List 16, 'User industries', Question 16.15, for a prompt list of examples of factors that might form part of the 'mix' in decision-making and List 17, 'Competitive climate', answer to question 17.51.)

13.18 Is this knowledge used in our marketing?

13.19 If so, in what way?

13.20 Have we linked benefits to the interests and responsibilities of different members of the DMU at different stages of the buying process and in different buy classes? (Relate to Questions 13.10 and 13.17 and List 2, 'Product/service range', Questions 2.27 and 2.28; also List 14, 'Analysing lost business', Question 14.10.)

13.21 Do we have any method for monitoring changes in customer and prospect companies?

13.22 Does purchasing responsibility divide at discrete points (i.e., size of purchase, unit price, value of contract, etc.)? (See Introduction.)

13.23 Where buying responsibility changes on value of contract, is there a tendency for a multiplicity of small orders to be given to circumvent the policy?

13.24 Does our knowledge of the policy permit us to take advantage of the situation?

13.25 Is there any action we can take to move buying responsibility into the part of the DMU that may favour us?

13.26 Do customer firms usually have a short-list of potential or approved suppliers? (See answers in List 16, 'User industries', Questions 16.60–16.62 and List 17, 'Competitive climate', Question 17.19 relative to this and next six questions.)

13.27 Who is responsible for drawing up the list?

13.28 How frequently do we fail to obtain inclusion on any short-list?

13.29 What reason can we attribute to this failure?

13.30 Which competitors appear on most customer and prospective customer lists?

13.31 How do we account for the frequency of their inclusion?

13.32 How can we obtain entry on lists? (Compare answers to Questions 13.26–13.32 with List 14, 'Analysing lost business', Questions 14.15 and 14.16.)

13.33 Do we have any knowledge of how members of the DMU prefer to be sold to (e.g., salesmen, catalogues, exhibitions, demonstrations, reference plant)?

13.34 Does our marketing reflect this?

13.35 How far are expressed preferences a reflection of status rather than the reality (See Introduction.)

13.36 Are specifications, when set, rigid?

13.37 When they are rigid, are the decision factors, considered by the member of the DMU with whom the salesman interfaces, strictly and only commercial?

13.38 To what extent can members of the DMU be persuaded to seek or press for a new or modified specification?

13.39 What information do we have on customers' evaluation techniques? (See List 2, 'Product/service range', Question 2.45.)

13.40 As part of our promotion, can we educate customers to use evaluation methods that favour us? (See answer to List 14, 'Analysing lost business', Question 14.13, and List 16, 'User industries', Questions 16.43–16.45.)

13.41 Is there a pattern in an analysis of business obtained (e.g., same type of DMU, customer purchasing practices, identical benefits sought, etc.)? (But see some suggested factors in List 16, 'User industries', Question 16.12.)

13.42 Can this pattern be applied to prospective customers or used to identify high potential prospects? (See Introduction to List 9, 'The sales force', and answer to Question 9.79.)

13.43 Is there a pattern of lost business which indicates wrong DMU identification, late intervention in the buy phase, wrong classification of buy class, or promotion of wrong benefits? (See answers in List 14, 'Analysing lost business', Questions 14.5–14.10.)

Appendix 13A. Short bibliography on purchasing

Because of the importance of understanding the buying/selling interface, the following short bibliography may be of assistance.

Blenkhorn, D. and Banting, P. M., 'Broadening the concept of industrial purchasing', *Industrial Marketing Management,* **7**, 6, December 1978.

Brand, Gordon T., *The Industrial Buying Decision*, Associated Business Programmes, London, 1972.

Brand, Gordon T. and Farrokh Suntook, *How British Industry Sells*, Industrial Market Research Ltd, London, 1977.

The Buying/Selling Interface, Industrial Market Research Ltd, London, 1974.

Cunningham, M. T., 'International marketing and purchasing of industrial goods', *European Journal of Marketing*, **14**, 5/6, 1980.

Ferguson, W., 'A critical review of recent organizational buying research', *Industrial Marketing Management*, **7**, 4, August 1978.

Financial Times, *How British Industry Buys*, Financial Times, London, 1974.

Ford, D., 'Developments of buyer/seller relationships in industrial markets', *European Journal of Marketing*, **14**, 5/6, 1980.

Hakansson, H. and Wootz, B. 'Risk and the industrial purchaser', *European Journal of Marketing*, **9**, 1975.

Hiller, T. J., 'Decision making in the corporate industrial buying process', *Industrial Marketing Management*, **4**, 1975.

Marketing Science Institute, *Industrial Buying and Creative Marketing*, Allyn & Bacon, Boston, 1967. This is the seminal work on the subject.

Sheth, J. W., 'A model of industrial buyer behaviour', *Journal of Marketing*, October, 1973.

Staples, W. A. and Coppett, J. I., 'Sales presentation methods at three company levels', *Industrial Marketing Management*, **10**, 2, April 1981.

Webster, F. E. and Wind, Y., *Organisational Buying Behaviour*, Prentice-Hall, Englewood Cliffs, NJ, 1972.

Appendix 13B(i). Completed model of the buying/selling interface

	Collective decisions: decision factors considered		Individual (non-departmental): decision factors considered				Department decision: decision factors considered						External
Stage of buying process	Board	Inter-department management committee	Managing director	Other individual director	General manager	Company secretary	Design engineering	Production	Sales/Marketing	Research and development	Finance/accounts	Buying	Others outside company
1. Anticipation or recognition of a need or problem and a general solution		2, 4			2, 4			2					
2. Determination of characteristics of needed item or service				7, 8, 9				2, 3, 4					
3. Description of characteristics and quantity of needed item								2, 3, 4					2, 3, 4
4. Search for and qualification of potential sources of supply												1,9, 4, 6, 7	2, 3, 4
5. Acquisition of tenders or proposals and analysis												6, 7	
6. Evaluation of tenders and proposals and selection of supplier				1, 9, 5	1, 4, 9			2, 3, 4, 5				1,9, 8, 4	2, 3, 6
7. Selection of a contract routine												9, 4	
8. Performance feedback and evaluation				1	2								

How to use the matrix

Below are a number of typical decision-forming factors which will be considered by different managers at various stages of the buying process. Others can be added. To use the matrix indicate in each management function, and at each stage of the buying process at which they are likely to be involved, those factors they will take into account in arriving at a decision. Check that the managers concerned have the appropriate information on your product and that the method of communicating this information to the manager is effective.

Example. Purchase of a standby generator. The Board do not make decisions but an inter-departmental committee does. The general managers, other directors (finance and production), and a consulting engineer are also involved. Thus, at the evaluation of tender stage (6), the general manager will take into consideration price, delivery time and payment terms. Also at stage 6 the buyer will be involved and will be evaluating price, delivery, guarantees, payment terms, credit conditions, and discounts. Outside the company, a technical consultant will be influenced by performance, physical dimensions, reliability of the supplying firm, and back-up services.

Factors for consideration

1 = Price	3 = Physical dimensions	5 = Back-up service
2 = Performance characteristics	4 = Delivery	6 = Reliability of supply firm

7 = Other user experience
8 = Guarantees and warranties

9 = Payment terms, credit, and discounts

Appendix 13B(ii). Blank model of the buying/selling interface

Stage of buying process	Collective decisions: decision factors considered		Individual (non-departmental): decision factors considered		Departmental decision: decision factors considered		External Others outside company
1. Anticipation or recognition of a problem and a general solution							
2. Determination of characteristics of the production service							
3. Description of characteristics and quantity needed of the production service							
4. Search for and qualification of potential sources of supply							
5. Acquisition of offers and analysis							
6. Evaluation of offers and selection of supplier							
7. Selection of a contract routine							
8. Performance feedback and evaluation							

How to use the matrix

List typical decision-forming factors that will be considered by different managers at various stages of the buying process. To use the matrix, indicate in each management function, and at each stage of the buying process at which they are likely to be involved, those factors they will take into account in arriving at a decision. Check that the managers concerned have the appropriate information on your product and that the method of communicating this information to the manager is effective.

Factors for consideration

1 =

2 =

3 =

4 =

5 =

6 =

7 =

8 =

9 =

137

List 14. Analysing lost business

Introduction

It must be very obvious that, unless the reasons why business is lost is known, it will be difficult if not impossible to correct a fault that may be fundamental to the product/service or the chemistry between the firm, its personnel, and the customer. A careful and on-going analysis will enable companies in many instances to rectify the cause of the loss.

'Lost business' falls into two categories: business lost for products/services that have been quoted for, and business lost because the enquiry or the request to quote was not received in the first place. Not to be considered for an enquiry can stem from lack of 'visibility' or lack of credibility. It has already been stated that one of the few absolutes in marketing is that, if prospects do not know you exist, they will not buy from you. The first task in marketing is always to obtain visibility and preferably absolutely unaided recall. (See List 11, 'Non-personal promotion: methods and media', Fig. 11-1.) The 'Heinz Meanz Beanz' syndrome is something most firms could usefully aspire to.

To have received an initial enquiry but not be invited to go to the next stage of sampling, quoting (or tendering), or demonstration, if appropriate, cannot stem from lack of visibility. Here it must mean the vendor is not acceptable for some reason. At this point there well may be an image problem if the perception of the firm and its offering is that of a less credible supplier than the others selected. Once again, with an understanding of this situation it is possible to rectify the position. (See Introduction to List 21, 'Images and perceptions'.)

These aspects of lost enquiries/business should emerge if Question 14.1 is answered objectively, but if needs be it should be researched.

The analyses are difficult to achieve because everyone is defensive and even an objective observer may be reluctant to comment critically on his superiors, peers, or subordinates. One thing is certain: salesmen are the world's worst reporters on lost business. For one thing, they tend to blame 'price', as this is the one reason that excuses everyone—the buyer, the seller, production, warehousing, credit control. Yet, as will have been seen in List 2, 'Product/service range', Question 2.23, and later in List 20, 'Pricing', Fig. 20-1, while price is not unimportant, it is by no means always the dominant issue in a buying decision. Customers buy more than price, perhaps reliability, stock, service, image. The marketing auditor in using the list below must ask after each question: how valid is the answer? Where did the information come from? Has the informant any reason to be defensive? Some judgement of reliability has to be placed on every reply before it becomes usable.

Question 14.2, aligning reasons given with choice made, is often a good test of reliability. Where a lost order is reported as having been given to a higher-specification product which

138

on investigation is found to be similar, it is obvious that other factors led to the negative decision.

Questions 14.6 and 14.7, on communications methods, frequently produces glib replies. Here as much as anywhere we need proof that the messages are getting through to the targetted people at the right time, and that they are understood and believed. Failure anywhere along this communication continuum will inevitably lead to lost business.

The matrix in Appendix 13B(i) will have demonstrated both the complexity of the buying process and the multiplicity of messages needed for different members of the DMU at different times. Thus it is not a single message whose visibility, comprehensibility, and conviction needs to be traced but multiple messages to multiple recipients.

Many firms' response to lost business is 'we wuz robbed'. This may indeed be true if the evaluation techniques used by customers fail to take into account all the features and benefits of the product, support services, and commercial terms. Too few sellers ask buyers about the evaluation techniques, and thus never attempt to influence them. This was covered in List 13, 'The buying process', and is now slotted into a possible pattern of business lost in Question 14.13 and 14.14.

Question 14.26, on bribery, is a very difficult one to obtain a truthful answer to, at least in the more sophisticated markets of the world. It is even more difficult to decide policy for those countries and circumstances where the answer is positive. As was commented in List 5, 'Export marketing', Introduction, a check list must necessarily be amoral. Each firm has to decide for itself how far it will comply with customary (or even not so customary) methods of doing business. Whereas in the Middle East and many parts of Central and South America it is a recognized way of negotiating contracts, there will not be too much heartburning, in other countries the issue is not so easily decided. Just when a gift becomes a bribe no one has actually designated. Question 11.1 in List 11, 'Non-personal promotion: methods and media', regards 'gifts' as a legitimate marketing tool but relates to such trivialities as diaries, calendars, pens, etc., and the token gift to the Japanese visitor, and not to the £1 million bribe to the nephew of the ruler of a remote Arab kingdom.

The list as it is given assumes a total pattern of lost business. The pattern, however, may not be obvious unless there are some cross-analyses. For example, business might be lost continuously in the private as opposed to public hospital sector; in the north of Scotland as compared to South Wales; when a particular material is being used with equipment; in benign as opposed to aggressive atmospheres; and so on. Because there is not a total or obvious pattern of lost business, it must not be assumed that one could not be uncovered by analysing the material in a segmented as opposed to homogeneous manner. Question 14.28 concludes the list on this very fundamental issue. Without the analysis, the investigation of lost business becomes an interesting but not a useful exercise.

14.1 What reasons are given for the loss of orders or enquiries? (Compare answer with List 9, 'The sales force', Question 9.98.)

14.2 Do those reasons align with the choice eventually made of product/service or suppliers?

14.3 What advantages did the competitors have?

14.4 How did they express them?

14.5 Did we contact the decision-makers? (See List 13 'The buying process', Questions 13.4 and 13.5.)

14.6 Are the techniques we are using to get our message to members of the DMU whom our salesmen do not see effective? (See List 11, 'Non-personal promotion: methods and media', and List 13, 'The buying process', Questions 13.7, 13.8, and 13.43.)

14.7 Do they intercept the buy phase at the moment of each member of the DMU's involvement in the purchase? (See List 13, 'The buying process', Question 13.9.)

14.8 Does our strategy take advantage of buy class knowledge? (See List 13, 'The buying process', Question 13.11.)

14.9 Do our marketing messages contain the information that the individual members of the DMU require, and is the information expressed as benefits? (See answers to List 2, 'Product/service range', Questions 2.23–2.27.)

14.10 Was our offer the correct one for the prospective customer?

14.11 How do we know?

14.12 If it was incorrect, in what way was it inappropriate?

14.13 What evaluation techniques did the customer use? (See List 13, 'The buying process', Question 13.40.)

14.14 How does our product/service measure up against the evaluation techniques and against our claims for the product/service? (Compare answer with List 16, 'User industries', Question 16.45, and List 17, 'Competitive climate', Question 17.52.)

14.15 Which firms were invited to quote? (See List 13, 'The buying process', Question 13.30.)

14.16 Are they comparable with us in terms of offerings?

14.17 What were the buying motives? (Compare answer with Questions 14.9 and 14.10 above.)

14.18 What were the buying resistances?

14.19 Did the benefits we offered meet the objections?

14.20 What proof did we offer that the benefits sought/offered would be achieved? (See Fig. 2-1 in List 2, 'Product/service range'.)

14.21 Was the proof incontrovertible?

14.22 If not, how were our assurances expressed?

14.23 Were audio-visual and other sales aids used?

14.24 If not, would they have helped?

14.25 If so, were they relevant to the presentation?

14.26 Is there any evidence of inducements being offered to purchase?

14.27 Should we emulate these or report them?

14.28 Is it possible to discern a general or a segmented pattern of lost business? (See Introduction.)

List 15. Introducing new products/services

Introduction

The life-blood of all organizations must be new products or services. Indeed, most companies' genesis derived from an original (but not necessarily innovative) idea of its founders. However, there is among some managers a reluctance to accept that a once-new product or idea is becoming geriatric, or that any later development is an improvement over the old ways and materials.

New product/service search for most companies appears to be sporadic, undisciplined, without direction and focus, and undertaken by executives often highly unsuitable for the task, lacking personal and corporate imagination.

It is difficult nevertheless to account for the extraordinarily high rate of new product failures, from the highly publicized disasters of the Ford Edsel, Du Pont's Corfam and the tobacco substitute fiasco to a million unheralded mortalities.

The search for new products/services should be a constant on-going activity, ranking equal in importance with all other marketing functions, with the search area and evaluation methods subject to precise methodologies and criteria, as well as with the strictest disciplines.

This is not to say that a reactive or speculative approach will not also pay off. The methodical search for new products/services does not rule out entrepreneurial flair and opportunistic response, or the exploitation of an idea that has emerged from outside the search system set up.

It is so important to keep well in the forefront for consideration relative to developing new offers that the company should always work from inherent or acquirable strengths. Reference below to List 17, 'Competitive climate', Questions 17.7 and 17.8, will give an outline of the factors to be considered in a strength profile on a comparison basis. The company's own strengths on a non-comparable basis will already have been designated in List 4, 'Company performance', Question 4.1.

The list that follows is substantially in two parts. The first deals with the need for new products/services and the generating of new product/service ideas; the second with the markets the new products/services may command.

There are four product options that can be considered. In the context of the matrix in Fig. 15-1, 'new' does not necessarily mean 'innovative', but 'new' to the company. Squares 1 and 2 fall outside this list, which concentrates on 3 and 4. Square 3 is particularly interesting because, in looking for new product ideas, the question can be asked, 'What do our customers buy that they do not buy from us but that we could supply?' Because they are already customers, this represents a market resource of a strength that can be exploited. Question 15.6 could be the key to open the door to a whole range of suitable new

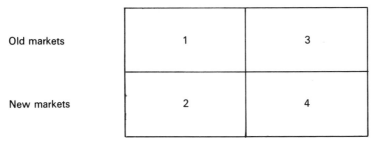

Old markets	1	3
New markets	2	4

Figure 15-1 Product matrix

products/services without the considerable investment in time and money usually necessary to acquire profitable additional offerings.

The fact is that an existing customer has already expressed a preference for the supplier, whether it be positive—a liking for the company, a high regard for its products/services or some rub-off prestige—or negative—'the best of a bad bunch'. The differential advantage referred to in the Introduction to List 4, 'Company performance', and Question 4.38 has thus been demonstrated to exist. It places the company seeking to supply a wider range of products/services to an established customer in a strong position to identify what the customer buys that the vendor could supply. The resultant extended product range may then very well have an application for other customers and prospects.

A schematic showing the preliminary steps required before actually beginning the search process and to confine the search to manageable proportions is shown in Fig. 15-2.

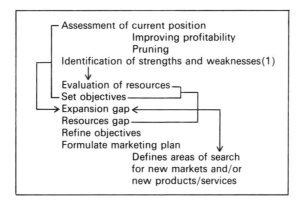

Figure 15-2 Setting the search boundaries. *Note 1*: See Fig. 1-2 in List 1, 'Marketing strategy and planning'.

Questions 15.1–15.8 should lead to a consideration of the present position and opportunities before turning to the new product/service decision. In particular, Question 15.8, which is a Square 4 approach, requires consideration as to whether a development proposed is not from the weakest position, i.e., trying to market a new unknown product (to the firm) to new unknown customers, as compared with, say, attempting to market new products/services to existing customers or existing products/services to new customers. Square 4 products are not based on any resource—market, technical, procurement—and moreover they usually draw away finance from what might be better opportunities. Square 4 is a perfectly legitimate position to occupy for firms that must have 'lead' products, but for most companies they would be well advised to look harder at the other options open to them.

The condition where sales approach reach the peak of the life-cycle is known as 'top-out'. Auditors should try to identify recognizable symptoms that would indicate a 'top-out' position (Questions 15.9 and 15.10). The list suggests that life-cycles are not necessarily immutable and under some circumstances can be extended (Question 15.11).

One problem bedevilling new product search is that companies do not always designate the parameters of the product/service wanted, most particularly how much volume/revenue/profit it is supposed to generate. A simple 'gap analysis' (Questions 15.14, 15.15, and 15.16) will show at once, if the business continues along its present path and growth rate, how close to the target figure it will be in a given period of time. ('Gap analysis' was included in the first check list: see Introduction to List 1, 'Marketing strategy and planning', Questions 1.7–1.9 and Figure 1-1.) It must then be asked, if existing products/services cannot fill the revenue/profit gap, what volume the new product/service must be capable of achieving. Thus, if £5 million must be found from a new offering with a total market of £2.5 million, this cannot on its own close the gap. Gap analysis at least gives the size of the problem and one important parameter in choice.

Question 15.24 will assist in setting yet another criterion for new product search—the commercial parameters, which must in turn line up with the gap analysis. The auditor will need to establish which items are irrelevant, which marginal and which vital as well as to add others which may be crucial to the company.

Given that new products are needed, then, it is the source of ideas and the methods of evaluation that become key. The extremes of rejecting ideas because they are new and of pursuing every idea is wasteful in time, demoralizing and dangerous. Discipline in search, discipline in evaluation, discipline in development, and, finally, discipline in exploitation are required.

Once more, a check list spawns another check list. There are many useful guides in check list form for new product idea generation and evaluation, and there are also systems for developing numerical criteria to achieve choice. The Qualitative Screening Process and the Product/Market Package are two such approaches.[2] For firms seriously engaged in the search for the profitable new products and activities for the first time, these should be consulted.

The final questions, 15.42–15.49, draw attention to what can be a useful source for new product/service introductions, frequently at low cost and with low risk. This is inward licensing. In a sense, the questions are the mirror opposite to those formulated in List 5, 'Export marketing', Questions 5.50–5.58, where outward licensing was considered. Before a licence search is undertaken, if an ordinate amount of time is not to be lost it is important to be quite clear as to the role of any licensed product in the product 'mix', the parameters it must fit, and the conditions of licence that will be acceptable. It is all too easy to fall into the trap of a quickly available glamorous product only to find at a later date that the licence contains many constrains or conditions which have been overlooked in the rush to get into production. Questions 15.42–15.49 seek to alert the auditor to the advantages and risks of inward licensing.

2. N. A. H. Stacey and A. Wilson, *Industrial Marketing Research*, Hutchinson, London, 1966, pp. 211–12, 260; *Planning a Diversification Strategy*, Industrial Market Research Limited, London, 1978.

15.1 What proportion of our present range of products/services are our own developments, licensed, traded, franchised, sub-contracted? (Compare answers with List 2, 'Product/service range', Question 2.4, and List 4, 'Company performance', Question 4.16.)

15.2 Do we need new products/services?

15.3 When will we need them?

15.4 Have we completely exploited the existing markets for our current range (Square 1 in Fig. 15-1)?

15.5 How far have we attempted, and with what success, to sell existing range to new customers (Square 2 in Fig. 15-1)? (Cross-check answers to this and the two questions above with both List 4, 'Company performance', Question 4.11, and List 22, 'Non-differentiated products', Question 22.17.)

15.6 What do our customers buy which they do not buy from us but which we could supply (Square 3 in Fig. 15-1)? (See Introduction.)

15.7 Why do we not make and supply these products/services?

15.8 How far is our new product/service search directed to new products for new markets (Square 4 in Fig. 15-1)?

15.9 Can we anticipate the conditions that will indicate when a product is approaching, or is in, a 'top-out' position? (See List 4, 'Company performance', Introduction and List 20, 'Pricing', Question 20.31, in relation to this and Questions 15.10, 15.11 and 15.12.)

15.10 Do we have a monitoring system for reporting 'top-out' conditions?

15.11 What plans exist for extending product life-cycles?

15.12 What plans exist for replacing declining products/services?

15.13 Have we set out and agreed the point at which, or circumstances when, we will eliminate a product or service (i.e., sales, profit, or stock levels, sporadic nature of demand, etc.)?

15.14 On a straight line projection, what level of business will be achieved five years from now?

15.15 How does this figure compare with the target set for five years from now?

15.16 If there is a gap, with what product/service do we propose to fill it? (The Introduction and Fig. 1-1 in List 1, 'Marketing strategy and planning', will give guidance on this and Question 1.7, the answer concerning the gap.)

15.17 What are the qualitative objectives for closing the gap (e.g., an aggregation of small orders, large business, combination of both, multiple products/services, full-line operations)?

15.18 Is our new product search formal?

15.19 How is it organized?

15.20 Who is responsible for it?

15.21 To whom do they report?

15.22 How frequently is our programme reviewed and success/failure appraised?

15.23 What is the consequence to those involved in new products/services search of success/failure?

15.24 What are the market performance and corporate parameters for the new product/service? (See Introduction.)

- Volume of sales
- ROI
- Anti-cyclical demand
- Sales to existing customers
- Marketing costs
- Inventory costs
- Value of sales
- Industries served
- Climate of competition
- Servicing requirements
- Credit costs
- Potential profit
- Anti-cyclical demand
- Compatability with corporate plans and aspirations
- Market potential
- Range spread
- Consumable/spares sales
- Evening out production
- Handling costs

15.25 Historically, where have successful new product/service ideas come from? (Compare answers with those in 15.1 above; List 2, 'Product/service range', Question 2.4; and List 4, 'Company performance', Questions 4.16 and 4.17.)

15.26 Can previous sources be relied on in the future?

15.27 If not, what system do we have for the searching (i.e., surveillance, market research, R & D, licensing, patent search, company or personnel acquisition)?[1]

15.28 What are our criteria for acceptance/rejection of a new product/service?[2]

15.29 What information do we possess on the market for identified or selected new products/services, particularly in relation to their location, segmentation and user attitudes?

15.30 What is the source and validity of our information? (See List 6, 'Marketing information: systems and use', List 16, 'User industries', and List 17, 'Competitive climate'.)

15.31 Are we monitoring future market changes for new product/service opportunities? (See List 8, 'Future market', Questions 8.18–8.21.)

15.32 Do we have a market entry plan for any new product/service adopted?

15.33 What resources will be allocated to it?

15.34 Is there a resource gap? (See Fig. 15-1 above.)

15.35 How is it proposed to fill such a gap?

15.36 What will the reaction of the competition be to the introduction of a new product/service?

15.37 Why should our customers buy the new product/service (benefits, patents, supply shortage, multiple sourcing)?

15.38 How acceptable will new products/services be to any intermediaries involved?

15.39 Will new products improve our procurement position?

15.40 Will they meet a demand in current or potential export markets?

15.41 How will they rate in terms of stability of demand, growth, marketability, lead-time to launch, life cycle, etc.?

1. The auditor may well get some guidance on the generation of new product ideas from Richard Skinner's *Launching New Products in a Competitive Market*, Associated Business Programmes, London, 1972, Chapter 3 and check list.
2. A specimen new product file will be found in the same book in Fig. 8, p. 31.

15.42 Would taking an overseas licence or cross-licensing produce new product(s)? (See List 5, 'Export marketing', Question 5.52.)

15.43 What level of revenue must a licensed product produce to make it viable?

15.44 Would a licence release resources—marketing and production—that could be redeployed more profitably elsewhere?

15.45 What role in the product strategy would the licensed product/service fill?

15.46 What are the product/service parameters a licensed product must meet?
- Will fill spare production capacity
- Will round out range
- Can be sold at lower price than competition
- Can yield higher margins
- Will release resources required for other product/services or activities
- Will compensate for lack of R & D facilities
- Will facilitate cross-licensing deals
- Will provide low-risk diversification
- Will associate use with a reputable, highly regarded manufacturer or brand

15.47 What conditions must be met and how far are we prepared to accept them? For example,
- Territorial limitation
- Methods of marketing
- Minimum sales or royalties
- Time limits
- Non-competition with the licensor
- Financial strength of licensor
- Licensor known in our markets
- Exclusivity
- Access to onward development
- No claw-back arrangements
- No minimum or down payments
- Willingness to have our names linked to the licensor's

15.48 What conditions do we require for a license to be taken?

15.49 Given that licensing is a method for new product development, have we a properly developed system for license search, and have the actions been allocated and scheduled and arrangements made for monitoring progress?[3]

---

3. It would be useful to cross-check the questions on licensing-in with those on licensing-out in List 5, 'Export marketing', Questions 5.50–5.58.

List 16. User industries

Introduction

This list attempts first to force an open-minded reconsideration of firms' markets, and then to review customers' policies, practices, and perceptions and problems.

All too often, markets are frozen into a pattern determined by the original product/service concept or the entrepreneur's or management's views as to the market configurations. Many opportunities are lost because of this rigidity in thinking. The spring balancers referred to in List 7, 'Market size and structure', Introduction, are largely associated with the small machine tool and lighting industries but were found to have wide application in abattoirs and tanneries, areas far outside the market conceptualization of the makers of the equipment.

In the final analysis, the accuracy and efficiency of the segmentations adopted and already referred to often in earlier lists can be judged by only one criteria: not the ease in selling into the segment; not the penetration achieved; not the image obtained; but profitability. That is what it is all about. Thus it is as well, early in this list, to compare the segments with the profit they generate.

Question 16.10 can be answered sensibly only if the auditor has already decided in what terms profitability will be measured and how. He will need to know the composition of the major cost factors such as discounts, promotional costs, inventory, and product/service mix. He should also ensure if the items are *costed* or *estimated*. A discrepancy here can well lead to an incorrect deduction from the analyses completed.

Question 16.11 draws attention to a frequently overlooked fact touched on in List 13, 'The buying process'. A firm's regular customers often have some common characteristic, either because of the original segmentation or because, in a sense, customers of this type select certain suppliers. If such a pattern exists it may provide very precise guidance as to which non-customers represent the best potential prospects. Some years ago the Stanford Research Institute showed the way to prospect identification by their profiling method, a technique successfully adopted by many British companies since that date. (See Introduction to List 9, 'The sales force'.)

The technique referred to there can be taken further by breaking down the market beyond 'regular customers'. If, in addition, its composition is grouped into sporadic, one-off, and lost customers, and prospects who invite the firm to quote and those who do not, and then the common characteristics of firms in each group are identified, it will provide accurate guidelines for prospective customers to avoid or to place on a low priority basis and, as with the suggestion in the Introduction to List 14, 'Analysing lost business', and in response to Question 14.28, it will be found possible to decide what action to take, if any, to recoup the position. This customer categorization is the one suggested in the Introduction to the book as applicable to a number of situations being analysed.

A general, somewhat cynical, view is that the requirements of all customers are half the price, twice the quality, and delivery ex-stock. While it is not suggested that such desiderata would not be appreciated, buying and buyers are more sophisticated than this. It is wrong but nevertheless common to assume that all customer requirements are known. Research frequently shows requirements that have not been appreciated by suppliers and indeed often not enunciated by buyers themselves, since they too have blockages and can easily assume that a requirement cannot be met. Questions 16.14 and 16.15 give some objective and perceptual items which in various combinations lead to a favourable decision.

But in looking at choice it is as well to point out the warning of a phenomenon that has probably been the cause of more marketing disasters than any other single factor: namely, the idea that in expressing a preference for one supplier or product/service the buyer is also expressing a satisfaction. He is not. Preference rarely equals satisfaction. The only statement the buyer has made is that he prefers a particular offering to all others; and, like the majority purchases, industrial and personal, an element of compromise frequently exists. The gap between preference and satisfaction, if it can be ascertained, represents the best opportunity to wrest business from a competitor or to consolidate existing business. Anyone who can close the satisfaction gap must succeed.

Question 16.28 is frequently answered in good faith but nevertheless incorrectly. Too many firms take the dispatch date as the comparison with delivery promises. The customer will always take the receipt date, a difference that may be a critical number of days or even weeks. For example, in the past small parts dispatched by rail invariably took longer to reach the recipient than those that were posted. Today the position is frequently reversed. Telling the customer that the consignment has been dispatched might appear to exonerate the sender from responsibility for the delay: it does not. The question indirectly calls for a reconsideration of transport and delivery methods, which is dealt with in more detail in List 18, 'Physical distribution'.

Question 16.32 touches on reciprocal trading and other closed arrangements, overt and covert. Proof of cost benefit can often unsettle such arrangements, but by and large these represent 'hard' market targets and are better avoided in favour of 'softer' targets which may exist. It has been said that it is an absurd exercise to bang your head against a brick wall, but it is lunacy to build one specially for the purpose. Attacking a reciprocally trading market can absorb far too much of a firm's resources, particularly marketing resources, without either the hope or realization of success.

The position map in Question 16.50 relates to the map in List 7, 'Market size and structure', Question 7.37. In the former it was used to show the realities of a price situation in terms of market requirements and purchasing. Here it is used to indicate the positioning of the company or product/service as perceived by the market. First mark the position in the appropriate quartile where the firm considers itself to be. This might be done by the auditor, or by consensus from within the firm. Then, so far as possible, compare this with the customers' perception of the position, if needs be by asking them directly through market research or (but not recommended) through the sales force. Any discrepancy reveals an incorrect perception, which calls for an image correction or educational campaign.

This assessment may well reveal that the company is living in a cloud cuckoo land with an unjustified complacency, or it could indicate a market with unformed or incorrect perceptions. Either situation calls for immediate remedial action, but getting the market's and the firm's view to line up does not ensure success. It is the optimum position (Question

16.54) that will produce the conditions of market leadership. List 21, 'Images and perceptions', Questions 21.18–21.21, deal with this point also.

Questions 16.60–16.62 turn to the issue of preferential or selected supplier lists, already mentioned in List 13, 'The buying process', and which will emerge again in List 17, 'Competitive climate'. The need to know if such a list exists and the conditions for entry are so obviously important that it can only be wondered why many businesses persist in attempting to sell direct without first obtaining 'club' membership.

The last four questions, 16.63–16.66, could provide an explanation for something that sometimes mystifies firms. While the terms of payment may be identical in an industry, some companies enforce rigid payment on due date and ruthlessly refuse settlement discounts on late payment, while others, unofficially at least, ignore late payment provided it does not become too onerous. Organizations can however develop tactful and pleasant, even if firm, methods of requesting payment when others are undiplomatic and rude. This difference between two companies both officially following the same policy can well account for success and failure with any particular customer, who will obviously favour the less demanding firm when all other things are equal. List 17, 'Competitive climate', Question 17.65, also covers this point.

16.1 Which are the main and subsidiary user industries? (This information will already have been compiled in response to List 7, 'Market size and structure', Question 7.10.)

16.2 What research/application engineering has been done to prove the accuracy of the list?

16.3 What are the main constraints on demand?

16.4 What are the main stimulants of demand?

16.5 Are there any other actions we can take to remove or distance the constraints?

16.6 Would new applications be opened up with product/service modifications, or changes in our commercial policies including price? (See answer to List 7, 'Market size and structure', Question 7.25.)

16.7 What are the total number of firms or installations that could feasibly use the product? (The answer to this question will be found in List 7, 'Market size and structure', Question 7.7.)

16.8 What proportion of these represents a profitable market target for us? (Compare this answer with List 4, 'Company performance', Questions 4.4 and 4.10.)

16.9 How does demand vary between the various segments of the market? (Compare answer with List 1, 'Marketing strategy and planning', Question 1.17.)

- Geographical
- Process or application
- Frequency of purchase
- Benefit received
- Form of customer organization
- Demographic factors
- Lead time required
- Buyer's job function
- Guarantee claims
- Cost per sale
- Industry or trade

- Size of customer company
- Size of order
- Psychographic factors
- Full-line or limited-range purchase
- Seasonal
- Order source (e.g., OEM distributor)
- Servicing requirements
- Value added
- Credit requirements

(Many of these are a repeat of the suggested segmentation criteria given in List 2, 'Product/service range', Question 2.2. See also answers to List 4, 'Company performance', Questions 4.4 and 4.5. The answer will also help with profiling referred to in List 9, 'The sales force', Question 9.79.)

16.10 How does profitability vary between these and other segments?

16.11 What characteristics identify our largest/smallest customers? (See Introduction and answer to List 13, 'The buying process', Questions 13.41–13.42.)

16.12 Can these profiles be used to direct the sales force to and from similar potential customers? (See List 9, 'The sales force', Questions 9.79 and 9.80, and List 13, 'The buying process', Questions 13.41 and 13.42.)

16.13 What job functions are responsible for (a) initiating a purchase, (b) deciding the product/service type, (c) specifying, (d) selection of the suppliers? (See List 13, 'The buying process', Questions 13.1 and 13.9.)

16.14 What are the major decision-forming factors—subjective and objective—in relation to the product/service? (Compare answers with those in List 13, 'The buying process', Question 13.10, and see Question 16.15 for some suggested items for consideration.)

16.15 What are the major decision-forming factors—subjective and objective—in relation to suppliers?

- Quality of product or service
- Size of operation
- Guarantee—length and coverage
- Delivery speed
- Price, credit, discounts
- Problem-solving
- Administrative efficiency
- Financial strength
- Quality of marketing
- Geographic location
- Links with industry
- Full-line operation
- Frequency of contact
- Servicing capability
- Support services
- Production facilities
- Technical advice
- Joint research
- Image, reputation, and track record
- Quality of management
- Packaging and transport methods
- Climate of industrial relations
- R & D
- 'Approvals'

(A fuller compilation than this is given in List 17, 'Competitive climate', as prompts for Question 17.7.)

16.16 Is it possible to assess how far the purchase decision was a compromise and how far the final choice falls short of the desired true requirements? (See Introduction.)

16.17 Do user industries buy direct or through other channels (e.g., distributors, contractors)? (The answer to this question should align with List 12, 'The distributive system', Question 12.50.)

16.18 What are the reasons behind their policy to purchase through one route or another? (See List 12, 'The distributive system', Question 12.50.)

16.19 Should we incorporate the alternative supply channels into our marketing systems?

16.20 Can we adjust our product/service or commercial terms to win business from the alternative distributive channels?

16.21 Is purchasing cyclical or seasonal? (See Question 16.48.)

16.22 Are there any actions we can take to reduce peaks or troughs?

16.23 How are orders placed (i.e., bulk with call-off, *ad hoc*, etc.)?

16.24 Which method favours us?

16.25 What adjustments must we make to meet ordering requirements of customers or to persuade them to order in a way that favours us?

16.26 What are users' lead-time requirements?

16.27 How does this compare with our lead-time quotations?

16.28 How reliable are our delivery quotations? (See Introduction.)

16.29 Are any actions required to improve our delivery performance, and if so what are they? (Use List 18, 'Physical distribution', in conjunction with this question.)

16.30 Are there any known customer requirements not being met? (See Introduction and the items in Question 16.15.)

16.31 What prevents us from meeting them?

16.32 Are there technical or commercial links between our competitors and customers that influence the market for the specified products/services, including reciprocal trading? (See Introduction to List 7, 'Market size and structure', and consult answer to Question 7.2.)

16.33 Is there any way we can counter these?

16.34 If selling to original equipment manufacturers (OEM), do they resell the products for end-user replacement purposes? If so, what proportion of our sales to OEMs are for this purpose? (The answer to List 4, 'Company performance', Question 4.4, will give total sales to OEMs, but it will be necessary to extract straight resale by OEMs from the total figure.)

16.35 Should we seek this business direct?

16.36 What would be the gains and losses of adopting this approach?

16.37 What developments are occurring in the user industries that are likely to inhibit or stimulate demand? (See List 1, 'Marketing strategy and planning', reference to vulnerability analysis and the answers to List 7, 'Market size and structure', Questions 7.17–7.26.)

16.38 What actions are we taking to avert or exploit the situation?

16.39 What services are required? (See whole of List 3, 'The service element in marketing'.)

16.40 What knowledge do the user industries have of directly and indirectly competitive products/services?

16.41 What is the extent of misuse of the product/service?

16.42 Can we correct this misuse by training or educational campaigns?

16.43 How does the user judge the end of the useful life of the product? (This question will have been answered in List 2, 'Product/service range', Question 2.45 and will be needed for List 17, 'Competitive climate', Question 17.53, and List 20, 'Pricing', Question 20.21, while the answers in List 13, 'The buying process', Questions 13.39 and 13.40, should be related to this answer.)

16.44 How do the criteria for judging the end of useful life of our product differ by industry, application, or other factors? (See the answer to List 2, 'Product/service range', Question 2.45.)

16.45 Are the criteria for judging the end of the useful life of our product the same as those applied to competitors' products? (Apart from the cross-references in Question 16.44 above, at this point it would be as well to ensure that the answers given in List 14, 'Analysing lost business', Question 14.14 and List 17, 'Competitive climate', Question 17.53, also correspond.)

16.46 If not, why not?

16.47 Is purchasing or specification influenced or decided by individuals or companies not part of the management team? Who are they? (See List 13, 'The buying process', Questions 13.2 and 13.3.)

16.48 How stable would demand be in time of depression? (See also Questions 16.21 and 16.22.)

16.49 Is there a requirement for hire or lease facilities, and if so can we provide it?

16.50 Complete the diagram showing our view of the firm's position and of its products/services and the views of the market. (See Introduction and use answer in conjunction with List 7, 'Market size and structure', Question 7.37, and List 20, 'Pricing', Question 20.3.)

16.51 On what information is the above answer based?

16.52 Is there a gap between our position and the market's view of our position? (See List 21, 'Images and perceptions', Question 21.24.)

16.53 What action can we take to close it? (This question will occur again in List 21, 'Images and perceptions', Question 21.25.)

16.54 Do either the clients' positioning or our own represent the optimum situation for us?

16.55 Should we try and move the market towards our perceived position or ourselves towards the market's view? (See Introduction to List 21, 'Images and perceptions', and Questions 21.24 and 21.25.)

16.56 What marketing methods are preferred by customers? How do they compare with those used by firm?

16.57 If they differ, why do we not attempt to meet expressed customer preferences?

16.58 What are usual media read/seen?

16.59 Are these reflected in our PR and advertising activities? (See List 11, 'Non-personal promotion: methods and media', Questions 11.31 and 11.33.)

16.60 Do we know which customers or prospective customers have short-lists or approved supplier lists?

16.61 Do we know the conditions for obtaining entry to the lists?

16.62 Can we meet them? (The answer to the last three questions should be compared with List 13, 'The buying process', Questions 13.26, 13.32, and List 17, 'Competitive climate', Questions 17.19.)

16.63 How stringent in terms of punctuality in payment do users regard our business terms? (See Introduction and compare answer with List 17, 'Competitive climate', Question 17.65.)

16.64 How does it compare with competitors?

16.65 Would an unofficial easing of stringency assist business?

16.66 What would such a policy cost the firm?

16.67 What are user requirements for shipment and/or packaging requirements?

16.68 How closely do our shipment/packaging methods conform to user requirements? (See List 18, 'Physical distribution'.)

List 17.   Competitive climate

Introduction

It is a rare industry or activity where competition can be ignored. The very largest as well as the very smallest of firms are all affected. Unfortunately, looking into competitors' activities is particularly hazardous, in that it is difficult, if not impossible, to be totally objective. Many views on competition are based on multiple hearsay—hair-raising stories put out by sales and service staff, trade paper rumours, and wishful thinking. If any section in this book requires the marketing auditor to stand back and to be moved by neither fear nor favour, it is this one. In each and every case the unwritten questions that follow every item are 'How do we know?'; 'How reliable is the information?' Also underlying each question is the evaluation of 'Why does our policy differ from competitions?'; 'Should it?'

The questions in this list can be augmented by reference to the competitors in List 6, 'Marketing information: systems and use', Appendix 6A. Competitor data are much more easily available than many firms imagine, from both direct and indirect enquiries. Interviewing competitors is not industrial espionage and need be neither feared nor shunned.[1]

In examining competition it is important not to be too parochial. While direct competition—comparison of equivalent products and services—is obvious, there is also that part of the market where requirements are met by totally different approaches. For example, a competitor to air filters and their components is the vacuum collection of dust and swarf on machines. Some medical treatments can be carried out using either electronics or pharmaceuticals; and, in this same field, disposables of all sorts compete with sterilizers and laundries.

Thus, the need is to see how the total requirement is met, not just the part that is satisfied by directly competitive offerings. Questions 17.2 and 17.48 cover this point.

Question 17.8, on rating particular aspects of the offering and performance with either a major competitor or with competitors generally, can be refined by using a numerical rating and indeed by weighting the various issues in relative importance to each other. The same technique was suggested for selecting an export market. (List 5, 'Export marketing', Appendix 5A explains the method.)

Suppliers rarely give much thought to how deep their 'visibility' may be in firms—both customers and prospects. The fact they are known by buyers does not necessarily imply that other members of the DMU will know them and prefer them. Marketing must penetrate further than the buying office. Marketing auditors should look at the answer to List 13, 'The

1. Aubrey Wilson, *The Assessment of Industrial Markets*, Associated Business Programmes, London, 1973, pp. 190–1.

buying process', Question 13.1 and ask if all the key members of the DMU are as likely to know them as their competitors. Question 17.18 focuses on this aspect of marketing.

'Break cost', referred to in Question 17.24, can be a profitable strategy. Basically it is to make the cost of switching suppliers sufficiently high to lock the customers in. Any uniquely modular system does this as the customer has to continue to buy the module to maintain compatibility, and the more he buys the more expensive it may become to switch. Thus the concomitant strategy may be low capital cost and high consumable, spare, or add-on cost.

The distribution of competitors' sales will frequently correlate with salesmen's or agents' offices. It is useful to plot these from competitors' literature—a quick and simple method of gaining some insight into the geographical distribution of business. Question 17.40 can often be answered this way.

Estimating a competitor's marketing appropriations, as is called for in Questions 17.39 and 17.45, may seem an impossible task. There is no doubt it can be very difficult, but some aspects of promotion are capable of at least rough estimation. There are published statistics of some media advertising expenditure, and this is also calculable by the onerous but accurate method of measuring advertisements, noting their composition (colour, black and white, bleed, etc.) and aggregating the expenditure by reference to that medium's rate card times the number of insertions. Salesmen's cost can be estimated on the basis of published survey data—in 1981 about £16,500 per annum including car and other expenses. Exhibitions are calculable on the same basis as advertisement but using stand size and position and organizers' charges, but a notional figure may have to go in for stand construction and fitting costs and manning.

Questions 17.59–17.69 again seek to distinguish what a customer pays for a product as opposed to what it actually costs him. It is doubly important in relation to competitors. Any differences that can be accounted for will negate an apparent price advantage. However, differences can be real but difficult to determine. The price of zinc and copper process printing plate in Holland was found to be directly comparable to, or even marginally higher than, British products until the enhanced scrap value of used plate was investigated, which gave a clear advantage to the Dutch product. Question 17.63 asks the auditor to look much more widely than apparent similarities and differences justify.

In any event, in looking at price it is always as well to remember that pressure for lower prices by comparison with an apparently lower competitive price frequently comes not from the buyer but from the salesman, where the method of remuneration may favour such pressure. The Introduction to List 9, 'The sales force', shows the arithmetic of such a situation. Thus, all questions on price need doubly careful scrutiny as to source and indeed motive.

17.1 Which firms make directly competitive products (type and range spread) or provide directly competitive services? (Detailed examination of competitors' brochures and catalogues make the plotting of this information simple if sometimes onerous.)

17.2 Which firms make indirectly competitive products or provide indirect competitive services? (See Introduction; some additional guidance in completing this question might be obtained from the answer to List 7, 'Market size and structure', Questions 7.5 and 7.7.)

17.3 What are their market shares? (This information will have been provided in the answer to List 7, 'Market size and structure', Question 7.14.)

17.4 How deeply entrenched are they in the market?

17.5 How do we account for their customers' loyalty? (This information will have been provided in the answer to List 7, 'Market size and structure', Question 7.16.)

17.6 Where in their operations are they vulnerable?

Resources they use	*Resources they generate*
● Material	● Products
● Personnel	● Customer loyalty
● Machines	● Goodwill
● Finance	● Brand awareness and visibility

17.7 What competitive advantage do (a) we and (b) the market consider our main and indirect competitors have or claim? (Consider the following, which is a somewhat longer list than that in List 16, 'User industries', Question 16.15):

- Product/service quality
- Delivery
- Geographical location
- Size of operation
- Protection—official and unofficial
- Financial strength
- Quality of marketing and coverage
- Approval
- Links with industry
- Back-up services
- Ownership of brands
- Packaging and shipment methods
- Licences
- Commercial terms
- Procurement strength
- Full-line operation
- Administrative efficiency
- Servicing capability
- Patents
- Production facilities
- Guarantees
- Quality of management
- Reputation
- Problem-solving ability
- Distribution network
- Technical advice/joint research
- Track record and image
- Climate of industrial relations
- Franchises
- Unique selling proposition

(Compare with answer to List 21, 'Images and perceptions', Question 21.8.)

17.8 How far do competitors' products/services compare with our own on the following issues? (See Introduction.)

Better/Worse

- Technical leadership
- Quality
- Performance
- Reliability
- Finish
- Design
- Adaptability
- Trade-in value
- Physical dimensions

Better/Worse

- Price
- Production facilities
- Packaging
- Shipment
- Life expectancy
- Energy/consumable costs
- Maintenance costs including down time

17.9 What were our sources of information that lead to the above assessments? Place an order of reliability on the information sources.

17.10 Rate the quality of competitors' management and management systems. (Relate Questions 17.14–17.17 to the answer.)

17.11 What stocks do competitors normally hold?

17.12 What stocks of competitors' products do distributors hold? (See List 12, 'The distributive system', Question 12.38.)

17.13 What are competitors' distributor and user policies relative to stock-holding?

17.14 Have competitors' performances (profit, sales, exports, etc.) parallelled our own and the fluctuations in the economy over the last few years?

17.15 If not, how have they varied, and how can we account for any disparity with our own performance?

17.16 What is each competitor's claimed major strength and weakness and reputation among users? How far is the claim justified? (Cross-check with the answer to Question 17.7 and compare our own view and the market perceptions with the claims competitors make.)

Competitor	Name	Strength	Weakness	Reputation

17.17 Are there any steps we can take to exploit their weaknesses or counteract their strengths?

17.18 How far beyond the purchasing department in customer firms are competitive products/services known, and how far are they associated with competitors by name? (See Introduction.)

17.19 Is there any evidence that our competitors obtain entry to short-lists or approved supplier lists more frequently than we do? (Compare answer with List 13, 'The buying process', Questions 13.30 and 13.31.)

17.20 Estimate extent of direct and indirect exports and list main export territories.

17.21 Are the major competitors known to do marketing research?

17.22 Is this conducted by internal departments or agencies?

17.23 What image do we have of the main competitors and how does it compare with the image their customers and non-customers have of them? (See answers to List 21, 'Images and perceptions', Questions 21.8, 21.11, and 21.12.)

17.24 Is there any break-cost element in competitors' marketing or product strategy? (See Introduction.)

17.25 Are our competitors known by name or brand?

17.26 Is there a brand that is a generic for the product/service (e.g., Hoover—vacuum cleaner? JCB—earth mover)?

17.27 Do our competitors manufacture for firms with private brands?

17.28 What services do our competitors offer? (For classifications see List 3, 'The service element in marketing', Appendix 3A.)

17.29 Is any part of our industry or activities likely to be the subject of official inquiry (e.g., Office of Fair Trading, Monopolies Commission, EEC)? (See answer to Question 17.71.)

17.30 If so, is our firm likely to be part of the inquiry?

17.31 Would we benefit by an inquiry into trade practices?

17.32 To what extent is competition from foreign sources judged unfair?

17.33 What individual, or joint action (trade association), can we take to rectify or modify the position? (See List 19, 'Industry contacts', Questions 19.4–19.7.)

17.34 Does membership of a trade association, professional body, or other organization limit our competitiveness?

17.35 What would the advantages/disadvantages be of terminating membership? (See List 19, 'Industry contacts', Question 19.13.)

17.36 What methods of distribution do our major competitors use? (Compare answer with List 12, 'The distributive system', Questions 12.28–12.31.)

17.37 What aids do our competitors give distributors? (Compare with answer in List 12, 'The distributive system', Question 12.65.)

17.38 Is a franchise system operated? (See Introduction to List 12, 'The distributive system'.)

17.39 How many salesmen do our competitors employ? (See Introduction.)

17.40 How are they distributed geographically? (See Introduction.)

17.41 What type and quality of salesmen are employed—technical, semi-technical, non-technical—in our application/industry? (See answers in List 9, 'The sales force', Questions 9.5–9.7 and List 22, 'Non-differentiated products', Questions 22.25 and 22.26.)

17.42 What is the competitor policy on the use of agents? (See List 10, 'The agency system', Question 10.56, which might indicate a vulnerability.)

17.43 Can we identify their agents?

17.44 Should we attempt to recruit them?

(The answers to questions on agents should be compared with Questions 10.53 and 10.56 in List 10, 'The agency system', but it would also be useful to complete List 10 as far as possible in relation to competitors' policies and activities.)

17.45 What are the competitors' promotion messages, media and methods and appropriations? (See Introduction and List 11, 'Non-personal promotion: methods and media', Questions 11.23, 11.24, and 11.25.)

17.46 What are our competitors' policies on guarantees and warranties? (This question has been asked in List 11, 'Non-personal promotion: methods and media', Question 11.52, but also compare answer with List 22, 'Non-differentiated products', Questions 22.20–22.24, and List 24, 'Product/service financial information', Question 24.41.)

17.47 What are our competitors' packaging and shipment methods and how do they compare to our own? (This answer will also be required in List 18, 'Physical distribution', Question 18.6.)

17.48 What competitor technical or commercial policies are developing or planned which will impact on the demand for our product or service?

17.49 Over all, does any difference in our policies account for any performance differences?

17.50 How far do competitors' products accord with an idealized 'profile' of the product/service? (Compare with answers to List 2, 'Product/service range', Questions 2.43 and 2.44.)

17.51 Are the purchasing decision factors applied to competitors' products/services the same as our own? (See answer to List 13, 'The buying process', Questions 13.10 and 13.17.)

17.52 Are our competitors' products used in a different way to that for which they are promoted? (See List 14, 'Analysing lost business', Questions 14.14 and 14.17.)

17.53 Is the end of the useful life of competitors' products judged by the same criteria as our own? (The answer to this question will require comparison with that given in List 2, 'Product/service range', Question 2.45; List 16, 'User industries', Questions 16.44 and 16.45; and List 20, 'Pricing', Question 20.21.)

17.54 What changes have competitors made in their products/services since they were introduced?

17.55 What reasons can be attributed for these changes?

17.56 How closely do competitors' products conform to official and unofficial standards?

17.57 What is extent of competitors' product/service research and development?

17.58 What is their history of new product introductions? Rate their successes and failures and give reasons for them.

17.59 How do gross and nett prices compare with similar products or services? (See Introduction and List 20, 'Pricing', Question 20.20, where this reply is again required; but also compare answer with List 2, 'Product/service range', Question 2.23, and List 24, 'Product/service financial information', Questions 24.28–24.29.)

17.60 How does gross and nett price compare with substitute products or services? (See List 20, 'Pricing', Question 20.12.)

17.61 What are the competitors' usual credit and discount terms? (See List 16, 'User industries', Questions 16.62–16.64 for a comparison and answers in List 20, 'Pricing', Question 20.12.)

17.62 Is there any evidence of hidden discounts?

17.63 Are there any other off-setting factors to take into account (e.g., trade-in values, low-cost consumables, free service, free training, long guarantees, etc.)? (See Introduction. Some off-setting factors will be found in List 20, 'Pricing', Fig. 20-1 and the accompanying explanation.)

17.64 What is the price history of the most popular/least popular unit of sale?

17.65 How do competitors' margins and credit terms to distributors and other intermediaries compare with our own? (See answers in List 12, 'The distributive system', to Questions 12.46–12.48 for comparison purposes; Introduction to List 16, 'User industries', Questions 16.63–16.66; and List 20, 'Pricing', Question 20.12.)

17.66 What incentives—financial and non-financial—do our competitors provide for their distributors?

17.67 Where did the information to make this comparison come from and how reliable is it?

17.68 What reasons can we ascribe for fluctuations in price?

17.69 Is price consciously used as part of competitors' marketing strategy? (See List 20, 'Pricing', and compare answer with Question 20.20.)

17.70 How do charges (if any) for different support services compare with our own?

17.71 Is there any evidence of price-fixing—overt or covert? (Compare with answer to Question 17.29.)

List 18. Physical distribution

Introduction

It is true that industry frequently goes to extreme lengths to shade every superfluous cost and design feature out of a product or material and to use the most sophisticated value analysis techniques. Yet the savings achieved are often thrown away in the physical distribution methods or packaging. An electro-submersible pump that had been value-analysed and redesigned to a lower, highly competitive but still profitable price was packed using a material and in a manner that absorbed all the savings achieved in procurement and manufacture.

In contra-distinction, if the total pack material and design and handling costs are considered, it might be found that an increase in material costs will lead to a greater reduction in handling costs or in the costs of complaint rectification. Packaging, packing, and shipment has to be seen as a totality.[1]

Products are often dispatched by perhaps convenient but uneconomic routes. Packing and transport methods can give a company a valuable market 'plus' if both are designed to meet customer requirements rather than supplier convenience.

Question 18.7 has important implications for goods moved over long distances, particularly internationally, and which are not time-sensitive. It is often possible, by transhipment and utilizing mixed modes of transport, to achieve considerable savings in total cost. 'Least-cost' route analyses are not often attempted but are always worth examining.

It was pointed out in the Introduction to List 16, 'User industries', and Question 16.28 that firms usually take dispatch date for comparison with delivery requirements whereas the customer takes receipt of goods as the effective date. This difference can be critical. There is no need for a supplier to be blamed for late delivery if it is the carrier at fault, but this will inevitably happen if customers are not informed of dispatch date and carrier. This is a simple action to take and in many cases defuses an explosive situation. It is necessary, however, for suppliers to be able to monitor the performance of their carriers and to devise a system to keep the customer informed of the position. Questions 18.8 and 18.11 cover these points.

While customers rarely object to a supplier's examining their handling and storage methods with the aim of improving services to them, few suppliers would ever think of undertaking this study despite the obvious marketing advantages it would bring. Question 18.12 draws attention to this point.

On transport methods, any compatibility between the supplier's delivery methods and

1. The term 'packaging' is used to refer to wrappings, covers, and containers in which products are held prior to use; 'packing' is the protective material for shipment. 'Packaging' often has a merchandising rather than a protective function.

transport and the customer's facilities and handling methods must stand the vendor in good stead. From a simple situation of a fuel tanker too big to easily negotiate the customers receiving area to the complexity of supplier–customer interactive computer systems, compatibility offers marketing advantages.

In relation to both packaging and packing, if they are viewed as an entity it is always possible that an improvement in material or design of either covering might remove the necessity for one or the other and thus reduce the total cost to the vendor and remove part of the disposal problem for the user. This double benefit is one that is frequently overlooked. Question 18.14 could well reveal an important answer in terms of reducing marketing costs and increasing customer satisfaction.

Suppliers frequently fail to consider how the pack is stored, used, and disposed of. All three elements are often capable of improvement to aid the customer's utilization, and anything that aids the customer must be of marketing value. Despite the sophisticated use of packaging as a marketing tool in the consumer goods industry, it still has far to go in marketing 'convenience' as well as products, and most industrial packs suffer with major deficiencies.

Good marketing always considers activities from the viewpoint of the customer, but marketers or indeed anyone in the vendor company rarely bother to investigate the problems caused by packaging. Not all firms have incinerators to dispose of inflammable waste, and those that do may be reluctant to put through plastic waste. Pallets, crates, and containers awaiting collection can cause storage problems. Questions 18.17–18.19 will demand that the marketing auditors consider these, important to the customer, points.

Another often overlooked aspect of packaging are the advantages inherent in enabling the customer to maintain better visual stock control by distant identification of pack and remaining contents (Questions 18.27 and 18.28).

A glance around any store room shows how frequently industrial goods and materials manufacturers fail to take advantage of the pack itself to convey an advertising message. It is useful to examine whether or not a promotional opportunity is being wasted, as might be the case. The answer to Question 18.29 will reveal if this is so.

All in all, both physical distribution and packaging offer splendid opportunities for improving relationships with customers and strengthening loyalties. Reliable delivery, it has been proved over and over again, is almost invariably more important than quick delivery. Indeed, the call for stock is usually only a symptom of disbelief of suppliers' delivery promises. Similarly, easy handling of products within the plant and easy disposal of packaging are both factors that will enable suppliers to obtain premium prices.

18.1 What delivery methods are we currently using?

18.2 What are comparative transport costs and times using alternative methods?

18.3 What are the reasons for rejection of alternative methods, and how do they relate to current conditions?

18.4 Have we considered establishing our own delivery service?

18.5 Is it possible to develop a co-operative arrangement with other companies not engaged in transportation or only transporting their own goods?

18.6 How do our transport and packaging methods compare with competitors on cost, speed, liability to damage, and pilferage? (The answer to this point will have been given in List 17, 'Competitive climate', Question 17.47.)

18.7 Have we attempted any 'least-cost' route analyses? (See Introduction.)

18.8 Are customers notified of dispatch on day of dispatch? (See Introduction.)

18.9 To what extent are late deliveries caused by delayed dispatches and to what extent by slow transport methods and handling?

18.10 Do we know when delays are caused by carriers?

18.11 If not, is it possible to design a system whereby we can monitor delivery time after our products leave the plant?

18.12 How compatible are our transport method, delivery system, and hardware with clients' acceptance system and hardware? (See Introduction; also List 22, 'Non-differentiated products', Question 22.18.)

18.13 Is there any way we can improve its acceptability?

18.14 Have we carried out a value analysis of packaging costs? (See Introduction.)

18.15 Is the pack material and the design the most efficient to withstand damage in transit, handling, and storage, by impact, pilferage, moisture, infestation, or temperature?

18.16 Would it be possible to standardize the shipment pack to reduce transport costs?

18.17 Is the shipment pack destroyed, returned, or re-used?

18.18 Would there be any advantages to us or the customer to change the shipment pack to another type?

18.19 How are empties stored? Can we redesign the pack to minimize storage space required by customers, or to make disposal easier? (See Introduction.)

18.20 How is the pack used (e.g., holds contents until emptied; fully unpacked on receipt)?

18.21 What is the average amount of contents taken on each occasion?

18.22 Would it be a 'plus' if the pack had a dispensing/measuring device?

18.23 Has the pack a second use? Could we redesign it to give such a function?

18.24 Does the pack material, size, and configuration take into account customers' views and needs?

18.25 Does the pack contain clearly understandable instructions and warnings for handling?

18.26 How long, on average, is the pack held in stock?

18.27 Can the contents be easily identified from the pack, including numbers/volume/value remaining?

18.28 Over what distance must the pack be identifiable? (See Introduction.)

18.29 Does the contents and shipment pack contain an advertising message? (See Introduction.)

18.30 What reporting system do we have, and what analyses have we undertaken, of customer complaints relative to delivery performance, shortages, damages, etc.?

18.31 Do we have a formal system for resolving complaints? Is responsibility for this allocated and monitored?

List 19. Industry contacts

Introduction

No business can operate in isolation, and for many the contacts industry can provide are a vital input to their information systems and sales opportunities. Industry in this context is the whole complex of customers, competitors, distributors, influence formers, associations, and government.

A company's image within its own industry will often be a powerful incentive or disincentive for customers to purchase from them. Regular, creative industry contacts can materially assist a firm in many ways by providing 'visibility' and conveying credible messages concerning competence, expertise, reliability, quality, technical leadership, and so on.

The idea that all competitors are enemies is both anachronistic and absurd, and the exchange of information with competitors and contacts regularly can have a value far greater than the time involved might imply.

It was pointed out in the Introduction of List 17, 'Competitive climate', that meeting and, indeed, interviewing competitors is neither unethical nor difficult; and whether such meetings are formal and private or informal and at some forum, the value remains the same. The Adam Smith dictum about the men of the same trade gathering together '... ends in a conspiracy against the public ...' may well still have some justification, but by and large associations of all types can and do accomplish an excellent job in promoting both their own industry and customer industry interest and providing internal industry information, market data, interpretation of government regulations, representation to government, and a host of other valuable inputs to a firms' marketing.

For services, the inter-personal network (referrals) is the single most important business source, and thus there is a strong additional reason for close industry or professional contacts.

Companies should consider the value of every industry group, as Questions 19.1, 19.2, 19.14, 19.16, and 19.18 suggest—whether this be horizontal, such as chambers of commerce, or vertical, such as for manufacturers in the same industry or a research association—and evaluate the cost and usefulness of each of them. Those who are highly critical of associations must realize that it is within the power of members to shape them to their needs in terms of services and information they provide.

Among the industry, contacts not usually considered in this context, because they are seen as a training or educational facility, are conferences, seminars, and other meetings. A training officer will evaluate these in terms of their training value. The marketing managers will or should see them as opportunities for useful industry contacts and sales opportunities.

As such, details on these types of functions (even those that have no direct relevance to marketing) should be circulated to marketing departments. Question 19.22 seeks to ensure that these important activities are not set aside as irrelevant.

Another often overlooked contact point are government and para-statal committees, ranging from 'Little Neddys' and BSI committees to *ad hoc* working parties. For example, the Department of Trade formed an *ad hoc* committee to examine how the numerical analysis services of the National Physical Laboratory could become a profit centre. At least two members of that committee were drawn from industry and obtained useful on-going contacts for themselves and for the NPL.

List 11, 'Non-personal promotion: methods and media', Question 11.1, had an item 'secondments'. This can be a valuable marketing tool for promotional purposes and equally valuable for developing and cementing contacts. Secondments can be from the firm to government or private organizations, and in reverse from government and other organizations into the firm.

Finally, Question 19.28 suggests that it is possible to create a forum for contacts if one does not exist. At one time an association of industrial advertisers was created by a media owner, and a society of long-range planners by a management consultancy.

Having said all this, however, it is also necessary to add that an inordinate amount of time and money can be wasted on industry contacts that often deteriorate into little more than 'talk shops' and eating and drinking sessions. This is an obvious danger to be watched, and a comparison must be made of the value that comes from industry contacts with the value that might accrue from using the same investment of time and money in other marketing activities or other parts of the information-gathering system.

Each firm should do an audit of its industry contacts and decide if they are adequate or capable of improvement.

19.1 List the relevant trade/professional associations responsible for our products/services?

19.2 Which trade and/or professional associations do we belong to? (See List 6, 'Marketing information: systems and use', Questions 6.30 and 6.31.)

19.3 Are the subscriptions justified by the services we receive from them? (Review and evaluate services offered and see List 5, 'Export marketing', Question 5.7 and List 6, 'Marketing information: systems and use', Question 6.30.)

19.4 Are there services available we do not use? (See List 6, 'Marketing information: systems and use', Question 6.30.)

19.5 Why do we not use them?

19.6 What services would we like which the association could provide but does not? (See List 6, 'Marketing information: systems and use', Question 6.31.)

19.7 Have we communicated this requirement to the association?

19.8 Who represents the firm at the association?

19.9 Do they hold any official position in the association?

19.10 Should they?

19.11 How frequently do they attend meetings?

19.12 Is the cost of the time input justified by the benefits the firm receives?

19.13 What disadvantages would we suffer if we terminated membership?

(Questions 19.11 and 19.12 should also be asked relative to Questions 19.3 to 19.13.)

19.14 Which trade/professional association do our customers belong to?

19.15 If it is possible, would it be beneficial to us to obtain membership?

19.16 Which general business associations do we, or member of the firm, belong to (e.g., institutes of management; institutes of marketing; chambers of commerce or trade)?

19.17 What marketing value does each one have?

19.18 Which research associations do we belong to?

19.19 Is the company represented on any government or para-statal committees?

19.20 Would it be advantageous to be on such committees?

19.21 Where do members of the firm meet competitors and government?

19.22 Are we fully informed of conferences, symposia, seminars, and meetings for both our own and our customers' industries?

19.23 Who in our organization is responsible for gathering information on seminars, conferences, and meetings relative to our own and customer industries?

19.24 Is the information disseminated in the company, and who receives it?

19.25 Who decides whether such meetings shall be attended, and who attends?

19.26 Would releasing staff on secondment to customers, government, trade, or other associations create valuable industry contacts?

19.27 Is there any aspect of our operations that clients may want to adopt and for which we could provide client staff training? (See List 3, 'The service element in marketing', Question 3.27.)

19.28 If no industry contact vehicle exists, would it be useful for us to create a forum for the exchange of information and general liaison? (See Introduction.)

List 20. Pricing

Introduction

Perhaps the marketing auditor's task comes closest to the financial auditor's work in consideration of pricing. Pricing clearly has critical profit implications, but it also has other equally important, if not so obvious, functions which in turn will reflect on profit. For example, the psychological implications of price in terms of the positioning of the product or service and the firm is vital in marketing terms; market share is unquestionably a function of price related to other objective and subjective factors; new product/service development and launches may well be totally dependent on the achieved price of existing products/services. Whatever price is adopted, it has to support the cost of the marketing 'mix'. Thus, getting the price right is clearly an important financial and marketing task combined.

Although pricing is simply one more marketing tool and as such was just a single item in the long list of marketing tools presented in List 11, 'Non-personal promotion: methods and media', Question 11.1, its importance and complexity is such that it demands a separate check list because pricing decisions have an all-pervasive effect on the company's performance. There are at least five clearly different approaches to arriving at price besides the ubiquitous 'cost-plus' and 'what the market will bear'. These are listed in Question 20.1. They are essentially marketing tools, not accountancy formulae.

As a marketing tool, pricing has a great advantage over almost all the others in that it is easier and quicker to change a price than to change a product or service, adjust an advertising strategy, design an exhibit, or alter a brochure. Moreover, the effect of pricing decisions is immediate. Pricing does not, however—and contrary to the much loved folklore of industry—mean price-cutting. On the contrary, it can as easily mean price increases. It has already been suggested in List 13, 'The buying process', Question 13.22, that buying decisions' responsibilities may change at discrete price points, and it may be advantageous to shift prices upward to move into the decision area of a DMU that may favour the firm.

In using price as a marketing tool, the marketer cannot escape the immutable formula:

High price = high profits = low chance of success
Low price = low profits = high chance of success

The marketer must position himself correctly along the continuum. To arrive at this positioning a great deal of internal and external information is required and the marketing audit can make a great contribution to the final pricing decisions.

It is axiomatic that good pricing depends on good costing, and while outside the normal ambit of the marketing auditor, it would do no harm to ensure that costing systems accurately reflect the internal position and that the inputs for costing are reviewed regularly.

Question 20.7 is in many firms a very touchy question should salesmen have price authority. On the benefit side, it gives the salesman greater standing in his relationship with his customers and enables him to be flexible and move quickly in response to a developing situation. On the minus side, as was pointed out in the Introduction to List 9, 'The sales force', in these circumstances price tends to descend to the lowest permissible level.

The case history of the firm marketing electrical insulation material referred to in the Introduction to List 9, 'The sales force', shows one approach to overcome this problem.

Questions 20.25–20.27 bring in the 'price and the perception of performance' approach, which seeks to place a monetary value on different attributes, the final price being based on the values that customers ascribe to the different attributes. Apart from the pricing implications of this approach, it also enables a number of other marketing decisions to be made with greater precision. Appendix 20A explains what it is, what it does and how it is used.

Question 20.29 has been anticipated in at least eight or nine previous lists. Anything to do with benefits, price as a decision-forming factor, price flexibility, sales and promotional platforms, unique selling propositions, and of course competition must impact on the way which a price is perceived and evaluated. In stating price baldly, the real price of a product or service is frequently overlooked or disguised, and this real cost might well be more favourable than the apparent price. The elements of 'true' price could include such items as servicing charges, consumables, life expectancy, disturbance, down time, availability of loan equipment, trade-in or scrap values, etc. Each significant item should be costed and offset or added to the price to arrive at the 'true' cost to the buyer on purchase and over the life of the product. A different series of factors will of course be required for assessing 'true' price of a service.

Presenting to a buyer what he really pays for a product is a powerful sales tool, particularly if an accurate comparison can be made with similar products or services. Indeed, if the components of the model are presented to the buyer and he is allowed to make his own evaluation, including those factors that are necessarily based on his judgement and unquantifiable, such as labour attitudes, but will also make a contribution to a decision, the resultant bottom line figure will have a credibility of considerable strength (see Fig. 20-1).

It is rare that inflation can be considered advantageous, but in terms of price movements it does offer a very easily explainable justification for price changes and helps break through the rigid price ceilings that used to exist and were difficult to penetrate. Conversely, holding price in the teeth of inflation is also a substantial marketing 'plus' without the unfortunate concomitants of price-cutting. Question 20.35 opens up this possibility for consideration.

Finally, Question 20.36 deals with the extraordinarily difficult question of bidding. The information a firm should have to bid intelligently is rarely available, but this is never any reason not to state the requirements as an ideal. Bidding is unquestionably as much an art as a science, and in assigning values to the variables involved in a bid, it is as well to check that such information as is available is used in arriving at the bid price.

```
Purchase price                                              £_____
Plus
    Disturbance costs
    Training costs
    Alternative use of money
    Consumables costs
    Repair costs
    Energy consumption
    Down times
    Space costs
    Maintenance
    Labour attitudes
    Possible add-ons
    Consistency of output
    Pollution control costs
    Accommodation costs
    Receiving costs
    Stocking costs
                                          Sub-total   £_____

Minus
    Tax amortization
    Discount or offset
    Trade in value
    Investment grants
    Recoverable waste
                                          Sub-total   £_____

Real price in money terms                  TOTAL    £_____
```

Figure 20-1 Model for arriving at 'true' price of a product

20.1 What method of pricing do we use?[1] (See Introduction.)

- Cost pricing—summation of chargeable costs plus desired profit
- Competitive pay pricing (service industries)—average or competitive salary levels
- Contingency pay pricing—fee based on acts to be performed
- Fixed pricing
- Contract pricing
- Value pricing—what the market will bear

20.2 How was the present pricing policy arrived at? Should it be reviewed?

20.3 Do our prices support our positioning policy and reflect market perceptions—actual and optimum? (Examine the positioning maps in List 7, 'Market size and structure', Question 7.37, List 16, 'User industries', Question 16.50.)

20.4 Will our prices support the marketing 'mix' we have adopted or will adopt?

20.5 How is the quoted price for an order calculated (e.g., individually for every order, individually only for large orders, standard list prices and discounts)?

20.6 Do market conditions demand a greater flexibility?

20.7 Do the salesmen have any pricing authority? (See Introduction; and List 9, 'The sales force', Introduction and answer to Question 9.21; and List 24, 'Product/service financial information', Question 24.14.)

20.8 If so, are the criteria for price adjustments clearly set out?

20.9 Who is responsible for monitoring price variances introduced by the sales force? (Cross-check answer with List 24, 'Product/service financial information', Questions 24.14–24.23.)

20.10 Would it enhance the salesman's role if he were given some degree of price authority? (See List 9, 'The sales force', Introduction and answer to Question 9.44.)

---

1. A brief explanation of these different techniques will be found in Aubrey Wilson, *The Marketing of Professional Services*, McGraw-Hill, Maidenhead, 1972, p. 136, or full explanations in specialist books on pricing.

20.11 What pricing tactics[2] are appropriate for achieving the marketing/profit objectives?

20.12 What discount structure do we and our competitors operate? (See answers to List 17, 'Competitive climate', Questions 17.61, 17.62, and 17.65; e.g., bulk; seasonal; settlement; retrospective; type of customer; i.e., OEM, contractor, wholesaler, end-user, other.)

20.13 What has been the annual average change in price of products/services over the last five years?

20.14 What were the reasons for these changes?

20.15 What percentage of the overall price change over the last five years has been due to product/service modifications?

20.16 Are the modifications as perceived by the buyers justified? Do prices as perceived by the buyer justify the modifications?

20.17 Would price-lining (holding price and reducing quantity or quality) be preferred to price increases?

20.18 When was the last price change?

20.19 Has it been justified to customers?

20.20 How do our prices compare with competitors? What accounts for this similarity/difference? (See List 17, 'Competitive climate', Questions 17.59, 17.63, 17.69, and List 24, 'Product/service financial information', Question 24.29.)

2.
- 'Loss leader' — Deliberately deflated price, usually to obtain 'first' order or to raise 'traffic'
- 'Offset' — Low basic price recouping on extras
- 'Diversionary' — Low basic price on selected products/services to develop a value image which 'rubs off' on total operation
- 'Discrete' — Price pitched to bring a decision into the area of authority of a DMU favouring the company
- 'Tie-in' — Price is conditional on the purchase of the tied-in items
- 'Discount' — Price quotation subject to discounts on a predetermined basis, e.g., time schedule, extent of commitment, magnitude of order
- 'Guarantee' — Price includes an undertaking to achieve certain results
- 'Price-lining' — Price of product/service kept constant but quality or extent of service adjusted to reflect changes in costs
- 'Predatory' — Price well below competition as a means of removing the realistic price applied later

20.21 Over what period do users tend to write off the product or the equipment into which it is incorporated? How does it compare with competitors? (This information will be found in the answer to List 2, 'Product/service range', Question 2.45; and comparison should be made with the answers in List 13, 'The buying process', Question 13.39, List 16, 'User industries', Question 16.44, and List 17, 'Competitive climate', Question 17.53.)

20.22 Is the amortized price comparable with competitors'?

20.23 Do any of the products/services under review act as 'loss leaders' to the total range? If so, which? (Relate answer to List 7, 'Market size and structure', Question 7.37.)

20.24 What evidence is there that 'loss leaders' bring in additional business?

20.25 What knowledge do we have of the attributes of our products/services that customers most value and prefer and are willing to pay for? (See Introduction and Appendix 20A.)

20.26 What knowledge do we have of attributes of our product/service that customers either do not value or rate as similar to competitors? (See Appendix 20A.)

20.27 Would customers pay more/less to retain/drop any attributes? (See Appendix 20A and List 22, 'Non-differentiated products', Questions 22.32 and 22.33 relative to this, and also Questions 20.25 and 20.26.)

20.28 What cost–benefit analyses have been undertaken to demonstrate any superiority in purchase of use of the products/services? (Align answer with those given in List 2, 'Product/service range', Questions 2.23–2.25 and List 17, 'Competitive climate', Questions 17.59, 17.60, and 17.63.)

20.29 Have any 'true' product/service price analyses been conducted? (See Fig. 20-1 and Introduction to List 2, 'Product/service range', and Question 2.23.)

20.30 Do our selling and promotional platforms reflect any benefits inherent in the total cost analysis? (The answer to this question will have been given in List 2, 'Product/service range', Question 2.28, List 9, 'The sales force', Question 9.43 relative to sales platform, and List 11, 'Non-personal promotion: methods and media', Question 11.33.)

20.31 Is it possible to evaluate our product/service position on the life-cycle? (See List 4, 'Company performance', Introduction and List 15, 'Introducing new products/services', Questions 15.9–15.12.)

20.32 Should price strategy reflect the product/service position along the life-cycle?

20.33 Would a change in price extend the life-cycle?

20.34 Do our prices move in line with/behind/ahead of inflation? (See Introduction.)

20.35 Can we justify/exploit inflation induced price changes?

20.36 What information is sought and used in bidding (e.g., estimate of direct costs, amount of past successful bids, average of all bids, identification of bidders, amount of individual bids, each bid as a percentage of own direct cost estimates, estimate of each bidder's work load)? (See Introduction.)

20.37 In setting price, do we consider its impact on others (besides customers) who may influence our performance? (See List 21, 'Images and perceptions', Question 21.29, for the various 'publics' that must be considered in setting price.)

Appendix 20A. Price and the perception of performance

Pricing is rarely seen or used as part of the total marketing effort. Generally, it is simply associated with such primitive techniques as price-cutting, price-lining and discrete pricing. The market in which price relates to a whole range of marketing devices and a product's own attributes has never been subjected to intense study and discussion.

Price is arrived at by an amalgam of cost accounting and a feeling as to what the market will bear, the main reference point being the cost of production and marketing. But production of what? Even a standard product like a screw has a number of variables which, although not part of the product, are nevertheless bought with it and indeed might well distinguish otherwise indistinguishable products.

The customers always buy more than just a product or service even if they cannot always sort out the various components of the purchased item. Generally speaking, little conscious thought is given by the customer to packaging, but its influence is unquestionable.

The personal buyer, as opposed to the industrial buyer, is even less aware of his attitudes to and perception of a supplier (image), but there is no doubt that the most intangible of market factors—image—plays a major role in decision-forming in individual purchasing.

Whether products are identical or wholly dissimilar, their characteristics and accompanying attributes do not rank equally in value in the eyes of the purchaser—nor, indeed, is the order of values likely to remain the same.

For example, a same-day developing and printing service for film would have a very high value for a short-stay tourist who wished to see how successful his photography had been while he still had the chance of re-taking the pictures. That same person at home would place a totally different value on such a service. To take another example, the name of a known and respected company on an untried product would have far less value in a repeat purchase.

Thus, in calculating a price it would be of considerable help to marketing men if they could obtain some insight into how much and under what circumstances the customer would be prepared to pay for given attributes. Moreover, such knowledge would make a contribution to product development far greater than conventional research can achieve.

Dr Irvin Gross, head of the marketing research department of the Du Pont Corporation, has completed a number of pioneer and, in marketing terms, exciting studies of the relationship between price and the perception of value.

Dr Gross's approach is, first, to identify attributes important to the buyer which are tangible and are part of the total product or service offer—quality, delivery, back-up service, company reputation. A 'trade-off analysis' is then made. Respondents are asked to consider a situation where all the factors are offered at a high level, but the suppliers, faced with increasing costs, will eliminate one attribute rather than raise the price (Questions 20.25–20.27.)

The respondent is then invited to state which features he would prefer to be kept and the strength of this preference. A number of additional pairs of attribute sacrifices are also given for ranking. Values are then assigned by respondents to the price difference they would tolerate to retain the higher level of performance of each feature. Figure 20-2 shows the pattern revealed for one product.

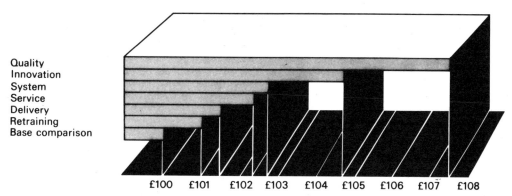

Figure 20-2 How much will buyers pay for a particular attribute?

Of course, establishing a price premium that customers would pay does not necessarily indicate they would buy any particular supplier's offering. The customers will have some knowledge of the market, however imperfect, and they will make a comparison between different suppliers, products, and services.

If an attribute is highly valued, it will not necessarily rate a price premium if a competitor's product feature is perceived as of equal quality.

The premium price a customer is prepared to pay is compounded by his perception of the value of the attribute and relative performance of the competitors' brands.

Applying this in a British market for reprography equipment, the attributes identified are consistency of quality of output, life expectancy, fast repair service and availability of loan equipment, reputation of company, staff training and stocks, and quick delivery of consumables. The consensus of value showing the percentage increase in price that would be tolerable to retain each attribute was in many respects similar to the results shown in Fig. 20-2.

The precision of the figures in the diagram does require comment. It would, for example, look quite different if the respondents had been solely purchasing officers, with the 'accountancy' factors such as 'life expectancy' rating far higher than technical items such as 'staff training'. Conversely, reprography or print managers placed a far higher value on consistency of output or loan equipment than on life expectancy. Irrespective of job function, there is a tendency to underrate intangible attributes such as 'company reputation', which other research has shown to be more important than respondents will overtly admit. Thus, in using Gross's tool it is necessary to examine results against both the job function of respondents and the psychological factors that, despite adamant and constant denial, do influence purchasing decisions.

The implications of Dr Gross's works are not just related to improved pricing techniques. It provides other important aids. First, where market perceptions are not in line with reality the marketing task is clear.

Second, where low values are placed on important attributes the role of marketing communication is to change customers' values. Dr Gross issues a warning that it is easier to change perceptions than to change values, and before embarking on a campaign to change values the effort needed should be assessed to see if it equates with the advantages to be gained.

Third, for both product and marketing departments there can be clear guidelines for introducing new attributes or changing existing ones.

An understanding of perception of value is likely to produce far more successful product and surrounding attribute modifications than conventional research can achieve.

Fourth, the technique provides a new segmentation base. The product can be forecefully and more successfully marketed to segments where the offering's attributes are highly valued, which gives either premium price and/or improved market share not achievable in that part of the market where the attributes are not appreciated.

List 21. Images and perceptions

Introduction

Among a number of trendy words that have permeated all areas of intellectual interest, 'image' stands out as a succinct way of expressing an old concept. It has long been insufficient for a firm merely to survive in order to be credible in its chosen field of activity. Increasing sophistication in the buying/selling interface has led to a questioning of the mechanistic nineteenth-century approach to business, which simply accepted that if an organization existed there must necessarily be an economic and profit justification. Today a firm not only has the task of survival, it has to survive in a way that makes it credible to its customers, its employees, its shareholders, and others. (Some of these 'others' are listed in Question 21.29.) The trouble is that 'image' has been abused, vilified, and raped until finally it has become a slightly perjorative term of abuse like 'slick'. It is always unfortunate when a useful term and a useful tool is debased and mis-handled, because image sensitivity and image development are an important part of marketing; indeed, they are marketing itself.

Whereas few would argue about the usefulness of the image concept in consumer goods marketing, it has still to be appreciated that the perception that an industrial customer may have of a supplier and its products, or clients of the professional practices they use despite the lack of obvious marketing activity, impacts on decisions. The notion that non-consumer buying is wholly rational and based entirely on technical and commercial consideration is still held, although there is a considerable volume of evidence to show that this is not so. Throughout the preceding check lists there have been direct and indirect references to the image aspects of marketing. For example, all references to customer benefits include not just those that are measurable, but also those that are perceptual. In List 4, 'Company performance', the assessments in Question 4.1 are essentially the internal image of the company's strengths and weaknesses—a point that comes again in Question 21.26.

List 9, 'The sales force', Question 9.43 asks about the sales platform emphasis, which includes both tangible and intangible elements, while Question 9.54 refers to the company's reputation—a pure perceptual factor. List 11, 'Non-personal promotion: methods and media', Questions 11.28 and 11.49 refer directly to image factors; and List 16, 'User industries', Question 16.15 is related strongly to the subject. The position map in List 16, 'User industries' is a pure image evaluation. Thus it can be seen from these few examples how images and perceptions impact in many sectors of marketing activity.

In looking at images, it is important not to overlook the *industry* image. Frequently this will rub off on the individual firm, or can create a far more intractable problem if such an image is unfavourable. While it is possible to separate the firm from the industry, it is not easily or cheaply accomplished (Questions 21.9 and 21.10).

Images exist on different levels. There is the *current* image, an encapsulated version of how the market really sees the image subject; the *mirror* image, the way the image subject thinks it is seen; the *wish* image, the way the image subject would like to be seen; and finally, the *optimum* image, that is, the one that will help achieve the company's objectives.

A printer specializing in financial documents believed his image to be one of a 'large company, old established, using the latest printing technology and providing excellent service' (the *mirror* image). In addition they wanted to be seen as a 'caring company, responsive, specialized in City work' (the *wish* image). Research showed they were in fact seen as 'staid, monolithic, bureaucratic, not interested in small customers' (*current* image). What customers wanted, however, had nothing to do with these factors. They required 'speed, accuracy and confidentiality' (the *optimum* image). It can be seen from this example how images can clash and as a result blur. It is to these aspects that Questions 21.18–21.21 refer.

Any gap between the way the company or its products/services are seen and the reality is known as the 'image interval'. A major market objective must be to assess if such an interval exists, if so, its extent, and then to take actions to close it, either by moving the market's perceptions close to the reality or by changing the image subject to match up to the market's perceptions. List 16, 'User industries', Introduction has already touched on this, but Questions 21.24 and 21.25 re-open the issue.

However, a firm does not have a single image, since everything it is, does, and has creates its own image—the products/services, the premises, the staff, the vehicles, even the paper heading. This is just one dimension, and some examples, which are covered in Question 21.26. The other is that in image studies 'truth' in a sense is of no consequence. Whether perceptions are incorrect or not does not matter. It only matters how the image subject is seen, and if a sense of injustice results, then there is an image correction campaign to be undertaken, making sure the true situation is communicated to the sector of the firm's public concerned.

A final and important warning: images that are not based on substance invariably end up placing their subject in an infinitely worse position. There should never be an attempt to promote an image that cannot stand up to reality. It is better to have no image than a bad image. It is cheaper, quicker, and easier to build an image than it is to correct one.

21.1 Do we have a formal image objective and development policy?

21.2 What is it?

21.3 Is it relevant in the light of today's business conditions?

21.4 Assess the degree of image sensitivity both throughout the firm and particularly among those members of the firm and that part of the firm (e.g., premises, vehicles, paper heading, etc.) that interface with the customers.

21.5 Who in the company is responsible for image development?

21.6 How substantial a part of the job activity does this represent?

21.7 Should the time devoted to image development be increased/decreased?

21.8 What are the images of our competitors? (See List 17, 'Competitive climate', Questions 17.7 and 17.23.)

21.9 What is the image of our industry? (See Introduction.)

21.10 Does it represent the industry's own view of how it is seen, or is it an independent assessment?

21.11 How far does the industry image impact on our own and on competitors' images favourably/unfavourably? (Compare answer in this and the next question with List 17, 'Competitive climate', Question 17.23.)

21.12 Does the industry image affect competitors differently from ourselves?

21.13 If so, why and in what way?

21.14 Are we as a company, or our products and brands, 'visible'? (See List 4, 'Company performance', Introduction and the response to Question 4.34, and List 11, 'Non-personal promotion: methods and media', Introduction, particularly Fig. 11-1 and Question 11.49.)

21.15 Would visibility be achieved with aided recall?

21.16 What part of the image perceptions are based on direct experience of company or reputation?

21.17 What evidence exists to support the answers to the previous six questions?

The next six questions should be applied to the following key market groups:
- Regular customers
- Sporadic customers
- One-off customers
- Potential customers where quotations have failed
- Potential customers where we have not been invited to quote

(See Introduction to the book and List 16, 'User industries', Introduction.)

21.18 How do we think we are perceived by the various publics listed in Question 21.29 (*mirror image*)?

21.19 How are we actually perceived by the various publics (*current image*)?

21.20 How would we wish to be perceived by the various publics (*wish image*)?

21.21 What image is likely to assist most in achieving our objectives (*optimum image*)?

21.22 What reasons can be ascribed to any variation between the images?

21.23 What actions are required to achieve the optimum image?

21.24 How far does reality of our operations match up with our image and the optimum image? (See Introduction and List 16, 'User industries', Question 16.52.)

21.25 What actions must be taken to close any gap between the image and the reality? (Correlate answer with List 16, 'User industries', Question 16.55.)

21.26 What is the image of the different aspects of the firms' products/services and operations? (See also items in List 16, 'User industries' in Question 16.15.) For example:

- Delivery capability
- Quality
- Price
- Services
- Technical capability
- Performance history
- Production facilities
- Aid and advice
- Control systems
- Reputation

- Financial position
- Attitude towards buyers
- Bidding compliance
- Training aids
- Communication process
- Management and organization
- Packaging capability
- Moral/legal issues
- Geographic location
- Labour relations record

21.27 How do the total and individual perceptions vary among the different members of DMUs?

21.28 Are the marketing tools we are using compatible with the image we seek to create? (See answer to List 11, 'Non-personal promotion: methods and media', Question 11.1.)

21.29 What is the image of the company, its products/services and operations as perceived by:

- Staff
- Suppliers
- Shareholders
- Competitors
- Our industry
- Financial institutions

- Government
- News media
- Local community
- Opinion formers
- Educational bodies
- Trades unions
- Referral sources

(See also List 20, 'Pricing', Question 20.37.)

21.30 How frequently will image benchmark checks be made?

21.31 What variants will initiate action?

21.32 How far are our promotional and personal selling activities deliberately intended to enhance our image? (See the answers in List 11, 'Non-personal promotion: methods and media', Questions 11.4 and 11.29.)

21.33 Should there be a change of policy to intensify image development aspects of our promotion and personal selling activity?

21.34 Would image development be enhanced by the use of specialist agencies? (See the answers to List 11, 'Non-personal promotion: methods and media', Question 11.35.)

List 22.   Non-differentiated products

Introduction

So much in marketing appears irrelevant to a manufacturer of a standard (non-differentiated) product. After all, screws, cables, chipboard, wire fittings, ball valves, plastic tubing, and drills, for example, made to BSI or other standards are identical in every respect. As a result, most companies marketing these types of products tend to fall back on a price response. 'Price-cutting', it has been remarked, 'is a technique for slitting someone else's throat and bleeding to death yourself.' A price response is a conditioned reaction based on a primitive perception of what customers buy. It is as unnecessary as it is destructive. Companies who feel themselves trapped in a market in which price is the only criterion for purchasing need to view their products and their markets in a much more creative way. There are techniques for removing the price emphasis in favour of values. As proof of this statement, many buying practice studies in the United Kingdom and in other countries have shown that something in excess of 60 per cent of DMUs would not move from their best suppliers for a drop in price of 5 per cent plus.

In one of the very few studies of the problem of standard product marketing,[1] it was pointed out that technical and commercial parameters of such products may well give an impression of a largely immutable situation which marketing cannot alter. The monograph emphasizes that the introduction of product 'plusses' can produce at least one opposite effect to that intended: a downward pressure in price on the existing products. A new improved chipboard for the furniture industry offered at the same price as the inferior one only had the effect of creating a demand for a lower price for the original material, since the industry did not require a better-quality product for a component that was not subject to mechanical wear such as a sideboard back.

Add to this somewhat strange phenomenon the fact that no financial or technical benefits accrue from using one manufacturer's products rather than another's and that there are no corporate or personal prestige factors stemming from purchase, there seems little opportunity to move away from price as a determinant in decision-making.

Differentiation will come not from observable or measurable product characteristics but from intangible factors which marketing must promote. There is evidence all round in consumer goods marketing that differentiation of similar products can be successful—petrol, detergents, light bulbs, and stationery are all examples.

There are some preliminary screening factors to be considered before tackling the marketing problem. First, there is the need to establish if the product is truly non-differentiated. The early Questions 22.1–22.7 deal with this point. Second, it is necessary to

1. *Marketing a Non-Differentiated Product*, Industrial Market Research Ltd, London, 1979.

see, even if it is non-differentiated, whether it would not be possible to adjust it in some way to create a differentiation, preferably innovative. The answer to Question 22.9 is intended to determine whether the standards are preferred or merely accepted. It is not possible to go below a legal standard, but nothing stops a firm going above it, or, for non-legal standards, below it. Essentially, the question is: 'do we know what the customer really wants, or does he buy what is offered because no alternative is available?' If it is possible to depart from the standard, then there is the possibility of a product differentiation.

Third, nothing in marketing can succeed without a knowledge of the buying/selling interface. Since non-differentiated products tend to fall into the 're-buy' class, the strategy to be adopted has to be to force a reconsideration of alternatives (see Introduction to List 13, 'The buying process').

Similarly, there has to be a knowledge of benefits that buyers either seek or would want if they were aware of them. Non-differentiated products and their suppliers do not necessarily produce non-differentiated benefits.

Fourth, one cause of price cutting, as has been shown already, can be the form of salesmen's remuneration, which may encourage them to offer reduced prices even when not asked to do so. The arithmetic of this phenomenon will be found in List 9, 'The sales force', Introduction. Before tackling non-differentiated markets, the marketing auditor should look hard at salesmen's remuneration method.

Consideration of these four factors will remove products that are not truly similar and also ensure that the efforts to achieve a differentiation for products that are similar are not negated by a lack of understanding of the buying process or by encouraging sellers to cut the price.

Question 22.17 draws attention to the fact that what is a standard and very unremarkable product in one industry might well be new and innovative in another. It is always a worthwhile exercise to look at the possibility of new markets for old products. The example of the spring balancer, quoted in the Introduction to List 7, 'Market size and structure', shows a successful approach of differentiating a market rather than a product. This essentially is the strategy involved in List 15, 'Introducing new products/services', in Fig. 15-1 (Square 2) in the Introduction.

From Question 22.18 onwards the questions inherently contain suggestions for differentiation. Questions 22.20–22.24, for example, call for a re-examination of guarantee policy— usually set by trade practices or tradition and as frequently completely out of line with what *could* be given, usually at little extra cost. An examination of guarantee claims and post-guarantee service charges will quickly show how far a guarantee can be safely extended. Apart from the values to the customer of a long and unequivocal guarantee, it is also a public affirmation of a firm's faith in products.

Question 22.26 highlights a mistake frequently made in the selling of non-differentiated products. Because there is thought to be little to say about products such as ball bearings, seals, duplicating paper, rivets, etc., industry tends to use order-takers rather than salesmen. But if you cannot differentiate the product, you can certainly differentiate the salesmen. After all, that is what selling used to be about before the pseudo-scientific approach became fashionable.

22.1 Is our product truly non-differentiated?

22.2 Would an improvement in the product force down the prices on existing products without guaranteeing increased sales on the modified product? (See Introduction.)

22.3 Are there, or could there be, any significant cost or other benefits for the customer in using our product as compared with competitive products?

22.4 If so, have we promoted these?

22.5 Would improved customer knowledge of the product and its use reveal benefits not obvious from the standard?

22.6 If so, can we launch a persuasive educational campaign?

22.7 Is it possible to introduce any prestige factors associated with ourselves or our customers?

22.8 Does our remuneration system for salesmen encourage price cutting? (See Introduction.)

22.9 Is the standard offered the preferred one? (See Introduction and List 2, 'Product/service range', Questions 2.17 and 2.18.)

22.10 Do we understand the buying processes for our product? (See List 13, 'The buying process', particularly Questions 13.11–13.16.)

22.11 What evidence do we have as to customer preference?

22.12 Can we go above/below standard?

22.13 What would the impact on price be?

22.14 Would the improvement in standard be seen by customers to compensate for any increase in price?

22.15 Would a lowering of standards be seen by customers to be compensated for by a decrease in price? (In answering this and the question above it would be useful to make a reference to the 'Price and perception of performance' technique in List 20, 'Pricing', Appendix 20A.)

22.16 Can we differentiate the product and the firm by a differentiation in marketing?

22.17 Can we differentiate the markets into which we sell? (See List 4, 'Company performance', Question 4.4 and Introduction to List 15, 'Introducing new products/services', Question 15.5.)

22.18 Would improved delivery method compatible with customers' handling facilities (or lack of them), commercial requirements, or supply or loan of handling equipment differentiate us from our competitors? (See List 18, 'Physical distribution', Question 18.12.)

22.19 Would a self-imposed penalty for unreliable delivery or products create a differentiation that would be meaningful to the customers?

22.20 What length are our guarantees and why? (Part of this answer will have been provided in List 11, 'Non-personal promotion: methods and media', Question 11.51; but see also the Introduction to that list and List 17, 'Competitive climate', Question 17.46.)

22.21 Could our guarantees be extended in length at nil or low cost to give us a marketing lead? (See answer in List 11, 'Non-personal promotion: methods and media', Question 11.53, and List 24, 'Product/service financial information', Question 24.41.)

22.22 Would guarantees extended in time and coverage have a value or benefit to the user?

22.23 In what way could this be achieved?

22.24 What would it cost as compared with the image and good will trade-off values?

22.25 What is the quality of the competitive sales force? (See List 17, 'Competitive climate', Question 17.41.)

22.26 Could we distinguish ourselves by the employment of high-quality salesmen? (See Introduction.)

22.27 Can we achieve a favourable dissimilarity by a link (acquisition, franchise, solus, trading, etc.) with distributors?

22.28 Would consignment selling (stock filling) be a marketing variant that would enhance our sales performance?

22.29 Can we link our product with another, perhaps original equipment, which will distinguish us (e.g., approvals, recommendations, mandatory use)?

22.30 Are there alternative uses for our product that would create a differentiation? (See example given in List 7, 'Market size and structure', Introduction.)

22.31 Can we particularize our product or the company by promoting a different image? (See List 21, 'Images and perceptions'.)

22.32 Have we isolated the technical and commercial attributes of our products and our firm? (See List 20, 'Pricing', Questions 20.25–20.30 and Appendix 20A.)

22.33 Can we place a perceived value on these attributes? (See List 20, 'Pricing', Questions 20.25–20.27 and Appendix 20A.)

22.34 Can we provide add-on services which would provide a product distinction? (See List 3, 'The service element in marketing'.)

22.35 Do we know the 'true price' of our product? (Compare with answer to List 2, 'Product/service range', Question 2.23 and see List 20, 'Pricing', Question 20.29 and Fig. 20-1 in Introduction.)

List 23.   Service businesses

Introduction

List 3, 'The service element in marketing', dealt with what services companies provide as back-up for their products. This section refers to pure service businesses. These range from simple refuse removal to complex financial or technical services. They have much in common with product businesses, but the differences that divide services from products are vital. The fact that there are so few cross-references to this list in the earlier compilations indicates the extent of the differences.

But while it must be recognized that services are indeed different, there are also, so far as the marketing audit is concerned, commonalities, and a large number of the questions listed in other sections, perhaps modified, will apply directly. Where there is a link between a product and a service the text will indicate this by referring to 'product/services'.

With the sale of a service the element of 'hope' is dominant. It is never possible to know precisely what will be received until the service has been rendered. Unlike a product, where the claimed physical and performance characteristics can be checked against specification or sample, a service can only be described, and the art of communication is very imprecise. How 'quick' is 'quick'; how does one rate 'effectiveness' or 'efficiency' of an accountant's service in absolute terms?

The situation is complicated by the fact that services are rarely pure intangibles, but often contain a physical element, just as products will often contain a service element. Similarly, although academics may talk of services 'perishing at the moment of their production', the reality is that services and their outcome can have a durability. While auctioneering and hairdressing are consumed as they are produced, R & D services can spread over years. It is a very useful exercise to categorize services, because it is then possible to compare services that are widely different but fall into the similar categories; to achieve a marketing cross-fertilization. The categorization technique, while not complex, is too detailed to be set out in this Introduction, but Chapter 1 of *The Marketing of Professional Services*[1] describes it and its utilization fully. Questions 23.1–23.5 deal with the categorizations and 23.6–23.9 imply the use to which the data might be put.

Many services, most particularly professional services, are severely constrained by the mandatory or voluntary rules governing standards of practice or ethics. Many professions reject tools of marketing that can be used because they are seen to be incompatible with their self-image. Nevertheless, management consultants use competitions; financial services offer premiums; accountants indulge in sponsorships. List 11, 'Non-personal promotion: methods and media', Question 11.1, enumerates many of the tools, every one of which ought to be

1. Aubrey Wilson, *The Marketing of Professional Services*, McGraw-Hill, Maidenhead, 1972.

considered by services businesses in auditing their activities. Questions 23.8–23.10 call for this reconsideration.

Most services comprise a 'core'—the basic purpose of the business or practice—and 'satellites', which are the peripheral and 'add-on' facilities. For example, the core service of a hotel is a 'place to sleep', but satellite services may well include shops, restaurants, room TV, telex, etc. Some satellite services are indispensable for rendering the core service; others improve the quality of the core service. It is necessary, since the quality and image of a service will be affected by the existence and performance of satellite services, that none should be introduced that will not be compatible or that might affect the core service adversely. This is covered in Question 23.11, but the auditor should return to List 3, 'The service element in marketing', and examine the questions posed there relative to the development of groups of satellite services which give added value to the core offering.

So far as professional services particularly are concerned, but also for many other types of services, the element of 'hope' referred to earlier means that there are many uncertainties involved in purchasing a service not present when tangibles are bought. A major part of the marketing task is to identify the sources of these uncertainties, which will vary according to the service, and then to ensure that the marketing messages reduce rather than increase the uncertainties. Similarly, professional and many other services are problem-solving. It is necessary to attack the substantive problem and to help customers and clients identify these problems. Finally, in regard to professional services the client buys professionalism. The marketing auditor must ask the questions concerning how clients define professionalism, and must ensure that the whole practice conforms to these criteria. Answers to Questions 23.12–23.20 examine these points.

The interpersonal network (referrals) is a vital source of business for many service companies, but all too many fail to trace the source of such referrals, fail to acknowledge them, and fail to market them. These three monumental omissions can easily be dealt with if they are identified. Most service businesses will find the best sources of new business are satisfied clients, whose value is greater than the revenue they themselves generate. Questions 23.23–23.28 cover these points.

The answer to Question 23.32 will often reveal a crucial weakness in service companies and practices where the task of marketing the service is separated from the task of carrying it out. Thus, an accountancy firm or a management consultancy may conduct a marketing campaign above criticism, but when the auditors or the consultants move into the firm their attitudes and behaviour frequently antagonize the client. This is usually in an attempt to prove they are not 'salesmen' but are highly skilled in other disciplines. Every service company must monitor the attitude of all staff from telephonist to the most senior members who interface with the client. Because a service company sells intangibles, the person is the surrogate for the product and everything the staff say and do will impact on the success of the service company.

Finally, Question 23.36 draws attention to the three basic methods by which a company marketing intangibles can approach its market. It is important to choose the correct approach for the service and market and for those who comprise the decision-making unit.[2]

2. A full discussion of the principles and practice of professional service marketing will be found in Aubrey Wilson, *The Marketing of Professional Services*, op. cit., particularly Chapter 3.

Questions 23.1–23.9 should be read in conjunction with the Introduction to this List.

23.1 How durable is our service (by way of example: 6 months = perishable; 6 months to 3 years = semi-durable; more than 3 years = durable)?

23.2 How tangible is our service (services providing intangibles, services giving added value to a tangible, services that make a tangible available)?

23.3 What commitment from the purchaser does our service require (long-term or fixed or both; short-term or flexible or both; optional)?

23.4 What degree of essentiality can be ascribed to our service?

23.5 To what extent is the service testable in more than abstract or qualitative terms?

23.6 Do other services that are successful share the same characteristics as ours?

23.7 Is there any aspect of their marketing that we can emulate?

23.8 Are we prevented from marketing by the codes of practice or rules of our profession or association, or by law?

23.9 What are the 'gains' and 'losses' of not conforming?

23.10 What criteria have been used for decisions on acceptance and rejection of the tools of marketing? (See Introduction, and List 11, 'Non-personal promotion: methods and media', Question 11.1.)

23.11 Have we a formal policy on the development of satellite services? (See Introduction.)

23.12 Can we identify and list sources of uncertainty among our customers and clients in purchasing our type of service?

23.13 In what way does our sales message attempt to reduce or eliminate these uncertainties?

23.14 Does our sales force and our non-personal promotion reinforce the messages designed to reduce uncertainty?

23.15 Do we market problem-solving or the techniques for reaching a solution? (This is the service business equivalent of marketing benefits instead of features. The question should be completed using the same format as in List 2, 'Product/service range', Fig. 2-1.)

23.16 Would our performance and acceptability be increased by a problem-solving approach?

23.17 How far are our clients capable of identifying their substantitive problems?

23.18 Are our staff trained and motivated to assist clients in identifying their substantive problems?

23.19 What criteria do customers and clients use to identify professionalism?

23.20 Do we conform to these criteria?

23.21 Are the skills of the representatives of the firm or practice commensurate with those of the clients to whom they are selling?

23.22 What percentage of new business comes from our initiative in approaching potential clients? (See Introduction.)

23.23 What percentage comes from referrals (interpersonal network)?

23.24 Do we know the sources of referrals? (See comments in Introduction to List 2, 'Product/service range', on indirect marketing.)

23.25 Do we have a formal system for recording referral sources?

23.26 Do we have any contact with the referral source, most particularly to acknowledge and thank them for introductions?

23.27 Are referral sources one of our marketing targets? (See also answer to List 7, 'Market size and structure', Question 7.32.)

23.28 What percentage of referrals come from existing clients? (See Introduction.)

23.29 Do we have any knowledge of the processes that clients use to select (a) a type of service; (b) the firm to provide it?

23.30 What criteria are adopted for selection of (a) the type of service to be utilized; (b) the firm that is to provide it?

23.31 What evaluation methods will be used after the completion of the service to decide whether it has been satisfactorily completed?

23.32 Are the service personnel/professionals who will actually undertake the service trained and motivated to deal with clients? (See Introduction.)

23.33 Is there a formal method of identifying and dealing with client dissatisfactions?

23.34 Is there a pattern of dissatisfactions?

23.35 Is the physical support of our operations compatible with the image we seek to project?

23.36 Is our marketing message based on (a) the methods or techniques of the service; (b) the reputation of the company or its personnel; (c) previous successful assignments; or (d) a mix of them? (See Introduction, and also compare answers to List 9, 'The sales force', Question 9.54.)

23.37 Is the approach appropriate both to the service and the market?

List 24. Product/service financial information

Introduction

Clearly, maximizing marketing operations requires more information than that referred to in List 4, 'Company performance', List 6, 'Marketing information: systems and use', and other calls for data through the book. The questions that follow are related to the two sections referred to above and extend some of the key questions. For example, Questions 4.3 and 4.4 in List 4, 'Company performance', call for annual sales by units and/or value of products/services, whereas Question 24.1 below adds information on margins. More importantly, however, this list calls for a review of precisely who within the company gets information. Many marketing aspects have implications for managers and departments not directly involved in marketing. Question 24.37 deals with stocks; and while it clearly concerns the warehouse manager, buying department, and of course production, it is also of some importance to marketing.

This list, perhaps more than any other, treats the firm as a total organism and not as a series of autonomous or barely related departments and activities. It is recognized that throughout the book the marketing aspect has been dominant—they are, after all, marketing audit questions—but the lists have never lost sight of the fact that the firm is an integrated unit, and no one department can operate efficiently or at all without the others. Thus, underlying what follows is the question not only of what information shall be gathered, but of who shall have it.

Questions 24.21–24.23 and 24.31–24.32 highlight a frequently occurring position where important financial data, which might well place a totally different interpretation on both the company's and on the marketing department's performance, are hidden by the reporting method.

Question 24.26, asking how data will be used, can and should of course be applied to all information-gathering, whether it be financial, marketing, production, personnel, or other functions. It is expensive in every way to gather data that are not used or are used inappropriately. The mirror opposite question to ask is 'what would the effect be of not circulating the information?' Yet another litmus test as to the value of information is to enumerate the actions that have been taken as a result of receiving it and that might not otherwise have been initiated without it.

Credit ratings are important to every company, and all too often remain unchanged despite the vicissitudes that customer companies go through. Few organizations have a regular checking and updating system, which could easily avert heavy bad debts. If the marketing departments and most particularly the sales force are kept informed of customer

200

ratings, they can adjust their efforts accordingly or, if appropriate, tactfully withdraw. Questions 24.34–24.36 examine these criteria.

In companies where stock is a vital ingredient of marketing message and operations, there is not infrequently a failure to distinguish the content by a number of criteria, such as current, modified, and obsolete—and, where deterioration can take place over time, recent. Question 24.38 might highlight a situation needing some adjustment.

As with so much that has gone before, the decision as to what data shall be collected, analysed, and distributed is very much related to the firm, its operations, and its markets. The questions suggest some items that will be key to most companies, but each firm must devise its own list. It is always important to emphasize the use of data rather than its collection.

Appendix 24A contains a summary and a possible format for financial control information. The auditor can extract those items he considers relevant to his needs. The data will in any event give some insight into many of the previous sectors of the marketing audit.

24.1 Are individual products/services and product/service groups, units, sales, and margins reported regularly? (See Appendix 24A.)

24.2 Are product line/service contribution reports produced regularly (e.g., price reviews, cost analysis, promotions analysis, product additions, product deletions)? (See Appendix 24A.)

24.3 Who receives these reports? (See Appendix 24A.)

24.4 Who decides who shall receive the information?

24.5 When was the circulation list last reviewed?

24.6 What evidence is there that the data are fully utilized by recipients?

24.7 What would the effect be of terminating the circulation of information to any particular manager or department?

24.8 Are annual sales contracts reviewed regularly to determine the impact of cost changes?

24.9 Who reviews them?

24.10 Are the data on which decisions based complete?

24.11 Do competitive pricing analyses and rationales available explain the differences?

24.12 Who produces them?

24.13 Are those who produce them interrogated as to the justifications offered?

24.14 Are variances from list prices controlled by appropriate managers? (See for example List 20, 'Pricing', answers to Question 20.7 in relation to this, and Questions 24.15–24.23.)

24.15 How are these and other variances reviewed? (See answer to List 6, 'Marketing information: systems and use', Question 6.34.)

24.16 How is the control exercised?

24.17 To whom are variances reported? (See answer to List 20, 'Pricing', Question 20.9.)

24.18 Is there a clearly understood policy on variances?

24.19 When was it developed?

24.20 Should it be reviewed?

24.21 Are special pricing arrangements, promotional prices and 'deals' reported as variance from list prices? (See Introduction.)

24.22 If not, how are they treated?

24.23 Does the system permit variances to be classified in a way that may disguise a position? (Compare with answer to List 6, 'Marketing information: systems and use', Question 6.34.)

24.24 Does product/marketing management have detailed cost sheets (including labour, material, packaging, overheads, guarantee claims, etc.) for all products?

24.25 If not, would there be any value in circulating these?

24.26 How would such information be used? (See Introduction.)

24.27 Is there a standard cost system in use for projecting profits?

24.28 Are prices compared country to country, regularly, sporadically? (See List 5, 'Export marketing', Question 5.3.)

24.29 Are they truly comparable? (See List 17, 'Competitive climate', Questions 17.59–17.71, and List 20, 'Pricing', Questions 20.20–20.22.)

24.30 Are receivables monitored by marketing management?

24.31 Are credits/returns collated and detailed on sales and margin reports?

24.32 If not, how are they treated in control data?

24.33 Are credits and returns monitored according to product and product lines and reason?

24.34 Is there a formalized credit rating system?

24.35 Who is responsible for operating and updating it? (See Introduction.)

24.36 Are sales staff given information on customer credit ratings? (See answer to List 9, 'The sales force', Question 9.94.)

24.37 Are detailed, accurate and up-to-date inventory reports available to appropriate marketing management?

24.38 Is inventory analysed in terms of current and obsolete products and related to short-term forecasted sales? (See Introduction.)

24.39 Are the expenses of all marketing activities (including salesmen and agents) planned and related to sales objectives? (Part of this call for information will have been satisfied in the answer in List 11, 'Non-personal promotion: methods and media', Question 11.16.)

24.40 Are all marketing activities formally evaluated in terms of effectiveness, cost, performance versus plan? (See List 11, 'Non-personal promotion: methods and media', Questions 11.16 and 11.18.)

24.41 Do we know the cost of guarantee claims? (See List 11, 'Non-personal promotion: methods and media', Introduction and Questions 11.51 and 11.53, and List 22, 'Non-differentiated products', Questions 22.21 and 22.2.)

24.42 Is there a recognized and enforced monitoring procedure to survey marketing costs related to marketing campaigns?

24.43 Who is responsible for operating it?

24.44 What changes have been introduced as a result of data emerging from the monitoring?

24.45 What does it cost to produce a proposal or tender?

24.46 Can the cost be reduced by adopting standard procedures, by simplification, or by computer and/or word processing? (The answer to this question will have been given in List 9, 'The sales force', Question 9.62.)

Appendix 24A. Model for required control information

Performance information	Report frequency: W = weekly M = monthly YTD = year to date	Standard	Variance shown by	Marketing director	Sales manager	Service manager	Chief executive
				Executives receiving reports: C = Control purposes I = Information purposes			
1. Sales							
Total sterling	W or M/YTD	Forecast	Sterling & %	I	C	C	I
By product/service	W or M/YTD	Forecast	Sterling & %	C	C	C	I
By region	W or M/YTD	Forecast	Sterling & %	C	C	C	I
By district	W or M/YTD	Forecast	Sterling & %	C	C		I
By nominated accounts	W or M/YTD	Forecast	Sterling & %	C	C	C	I
2. New accounts							
Total new accounts opened	W or M/YTD	Forecast	Sterling & no.	I	C	C	I
By product/service	W or M/YTD	Forecast	Sterling & no.	C	C	C	I
By region	W or M/YTD	Forecast	Sterling & no.	C	C	C	I
By district	W or M/YTD	Forecast	Sterling & no.	C	C		I
By nominated accounts	W or M/YTD	Forecast	Sterling & no.	C	C	C	I
3. Profits							
Net for company	M/YTD	Forecast	Sterling & %		I	I	
Company return on investment quarterly	M	Forecast	Sterling & %		I	I	
Gross margin	M	Forecast	Sterling & %		I	C	
By product/service	M	Forecast	Sterling & %		C	C	
By region	M	Forecast	Sterling & %		C	C	
4. Expenses							
Total sales and marketing	M/YTD	Budget	Sterling & %		C	C	I
By product/service	M/YTD	Budget	Sterling & %	C	C	C	I
By department	M/YTD	Budget	Sterling & %	C	C	C	I
By region	M/YTD	Budget	Sterling & %	C	C	C	I
By district	M/YTD	Budget	Sterling & %	C	C		I
5. Pricing/discounts							
Amounts of variance from planned prices							
By product/service	W or M	Plan	Sterling & %	C	C	C	I
By region	W or M	Plan	Sterling & %	C	C	C	I
6. Sales activity							
Total sales calls and orders to ratio	W or M	Plan	No. & %	C	C	C	I
By product/service	W or M	Plan	No. & %	C	C	C	C
By existing/new accounts	W or M	Plan	No. & %	C	C	C	I
By region	W or M	Plan	No. & %	C	C	C	I
By district	W or M	Plan	No. & %	C	C	I	I
By nominated accounts	W or M	Plan	No. & %	C	C	C	I

Performance information	Report frequency: W = weekly M = monthly YTD = year to date	Standard	Variance shown by	Marketing director	Sales manager	Service manager	Chief executive
7. Customer accounts							
No. gained by region	W or M/YTD	Plan	No. & %	C	C	C	I
No. lost by region	W or M/YTD	Plan	No. & %	C	C	C	I
Net change by region	W or M/YTD	Plan	No. & %	C	C	C	I
No. gained by product/service	W or M/YTD	Plan	No. & %	C	C	C	I
No. lost by product/service	W or M/YTD	Plan	No. & %	C	C	C	I
Net change by product/service	W or M/YTD	Plan	No. & %	C	C	C	I
8. Customer service							
Complains by type	W or M/YTD	Acceptable standard	No.	C	C	C	I
Complains by product/service	W or M/YTD	Acceptable standard	No.	C	C	C	I
Complaints by region	W or M/YTD	Acceptable standard	No.	C	C	C	I
Refunds and allowances	W or M/YTD	Acceptable standard	Sterling & no.	C	C	I	I
By nominated accounts	W or M/YTD	Acceptable standard	No.	C	C	C	I
Guarantee claims	W or M/YTD	Acceptable standard	Sterling & no.	C	C	C	I
9. Credit							
No. and value of accounts outstanding			No.				
Over 10/30/60 days	M	Objective	Sterling & %	C	C	I	
By product/service	M	Objective	Sterling & %	C	C	I	
Names of accounts over 60 days		—	—	C	C	C	
10. Advertising							
Sterling spent by media	M/YTD	Budget	Sterling & %	C	I	C	C
Sales promotion	M/YTD	Budget	Sterling & %	C	I	C	C
Public relations	M/YTD	Budget	Sterling & %	C	I	C	C
By product/service	M/YTD	Budget	Sterling & %	C	I	C	C
Status reports on functions literature, etc.	Quarterly	—	—	C	C	C	C
11. Market research							
Project completed	M	Plan		C	I	C	C
Projects pending	M	Plan		C	I	C	C
Sterling spent on research	M/YTD	Budget	Sterling & %			C	C
12. Product development							
Status of each project pending	M	Plan	No. of weeks	C	I	C	I
New projects started	M	Plan	No. of weeks	C	I	C	I
Projects completed	M	Plan	No. of weeks	C	I	C	I
Projects in market test	M	Plan	No. of weeks	C	I	C	I
By product/service	M	Plan	No. of weeks	C	C	C	I
13. Marketing/sales personnal							
No. employed	M	Budget	No. & %		I	C	I
By product/service	M	Budget	No. & %	C	I	C	I
By function	M	Budget	No. & %	C	I	C	I
No. of unfilled vacancies	M	Budget	—	C	I	C	I
No. and type of training courses	M	Plan	No.	C	I	C	I
In process	M	Plan	No.	C	I	C	I
Completed	YTD	Budget	No.	C	I	C	I
No. of personnel attending	M	Plan	No.	C	I	C	I
No. of personnel completed	YTD	Plan	No.	C	I	C	I

Conclusion

The lists are not complete—they never will be. The marketing auditor and others may well extend them beyond this framework and within which the marketing realization technique can be practised. The dangers of an endless list are obvious enough and were pointed out at the beginning. Deletion must be as important as accretion. Self-discipline will always be needed to avoid producing a *tour de force* rather than a down-to-earth practical aid to improving marketing.

It is fitting to end with the three notes of caution that have been reiterated throughout the book.

1. All answers to all questions should be examined critically relating the source of the information. 'How do we know?' is a vital interrogative. Folklore must be eschewed at all costs.
2. The way data are used is more important than acquiring them. The system fails totally and the time investment is wasted if the data gathered are not applied, are used only partially, or are used badly.
3. No action will occur as a result of the marketing audit unless every task is clearly allocated, tightly scheduled, and monitored punctiliously.

With the knowledge that every business has locked-in and hidden resources, only waiting to be identified in order to be used, the auditor should start and complete his task with the certainty that success must follow.

Index

Page references in italics indicate diagrams, tables or forms. A page reference followed by n indicates a footnote.

Training:
    aids, 189
    customers, 19, 21, 63, *113*, 123, 155, 174
    sales force, 92, *100*
    service staff, 18, 198
Transport, 60, 150, 153, 160, 161, 167–70
    (*see also* Shipment)
Trends, market, 52, 55, 82–7, 147
True image, 186
'True' price, 9, 176, 180, 194

Unique Selling Proposition, 10–11, 15, 116, 160, 176
United States: product liability requirements, 33
User attitudes and behaviour (*see* Customers:
    behaviour)
User industries, 149–57
USP, 10–11, 15, 116, 160, 176

Value analysis: packaging costs, 169
Value pricing, 178
Variance information, 52, 178, 202, 203
Vehicle livery, *113*
Viewdata, *113*
'Visibility' of firm and products, 24, 25, 30, 115, 116,
    117, 138, 158, 171, 187
Visiting services, 19, 21, 63

Visits, *112*
    to agents/distributors, 101, 105, 126
    to customers, 19, 20, 21, 63
Visual aids (*see* Audio-visual aids)
Vulnerability analysis, 3–5, 23, 78, 80, 84
    competitors', 160

Warranties (*see* Guarantees)
WATS, 32
Weaknesses:
    of competitors, 161
    of firm, 3, 7, 26, 143
    of marketing activities, 109
    of products, 29, 61
Webster, F. E., 133
Wholesalers (*see* Distributors)
Wide Area Telephone Service, 32
Wilson, Aubrey, 9n, 48n, 76n, 78n, 83n, 90n, 144n,
    158n, 178n, 195n, 196n
Wind, Y., 133
'Wish' image, 71, 186, 188
Wood, A., xviiin
Wootz, B., 133
Word processing, 90, 95, 204
World Index of Economic Forecasts, 40n
World Markets Workbook, 40n

Year books, 110, *112*, 177
Yellow pages, 110